Without A Second
Fundamentals of Vedanta

SHEELA BALAJI

EastWest Books (Madras) Pvt. Ltd.
• Chennai • Bangalore • Hyderabad • New Delhi

EastWest Books (Madras) Pvt. Ltd.,
571, Poonamalle High Road, Aminjikarai, Chennai - 600 029.
3-5-1108, Maruti Complex, II Floor, Narayanaguda, Hyderabad - 500 029.
53/2, Bull Temple Road, Basavangudi, Bangalore - 560 019.
A-10, Lower Ground Floor, Lajpat Nagar III, New Delhi - 110 024.

Copyright © 2005 Sheela Balaji

Price Rs. 250/-

ISBN : 81-88661-30-9

Book design:
J. Menon, www.grantha.com

Printed at :
Sri Venkatesa Printing House,
Chennai 600 026 E.mail: saicure@vsnl.com

Published by
EastWest Books (Madras) Pvt. Ltd
571, P.H. Road, Aminjikarai, Chennai - 600 029.
E.mail: ewb@vsnl.com

Contents

Foreword vii
Preface ix
Introduction xvii
1. Limitless Existence Consciousness 1
2. Real (*Satyam*) and Dependent-real (*Mithya*) 11
3. Subjective Perception 14
4. Orders of Reality 19
5. Self Conscious Being, the Knower 21
6. Individual I and Universal Consciousness 31
7. The Need for Sacred Texts 38
8. Validity of the Sacred Texts 41
9. The Sacred Texts are Valid means of Knowledge 46
10. Beyond the Senses and the Mind 51
11. Many Texts and Interpretations 55
12. The Sacred Texts are Dependent-reals 60
13. Sentient and Insentient 66
14. Origin of Ignorance 70
15. Cause and Effect 72
16. Creator and Creation 77
17. Is Creation an Action 83

18. The World after Knowledge	87
19. Projection and Superimposition	89
20. Reality of Superimposition	96
21. The Cause of Projection	98
22. *Maya's* Veiling Power	101
23. *Maya's* Ontological Status	106
24. *Maya* and the Limitless One – The Connection	107
25. *Maya* and the Individual Mind	120
26. Individual Understanding	125
27. Many Minds but One Consciousness	127
28. Helpless Individual	129
29. The Importance of a Master	134
30. Are the Sacred Texts Second Hand Knowledge	139
31. Can the Self be known	148
32. Is Without a Second a Tautology	152
33. Fate and Suffering	155
34. The Limitless One and God	159
35. Compassionate God in Heaven	165
36. The One without Attributes	170
37. Is Creation a part of God	174
38. Is God affected by the Creation	177

39. The Problem of Nothing-ness	185
40. Mystic Experience and Knowledge	194
41. The Role of Forms and Rituals	198
42. The Ideal Seeker of Truth	202
43. What does Death mean for the Wise	214
44. For Those who do not Know	217
45. The Wonder that is Without a Second	219
Afterword	224
The Story of the Eighteenth Elephant	232
Glossary	234

Foreword
by Swami Dayananda Saraswati

"Without a Second" is a book that unfolds Vedanta without "quotes" and usual Sanskrit words. It is an ideal book for gaining the vision of the Whole, the subject-matter of Vedanta. Even for one who has read a lot of books, with and without the help of a teacher, this book will be found very revealing — rewarding. Smt. Sheela Balaji, the author, has identified herself with a seeker and

raised all those questions which remain unanswered generally and answered them in detail with clarity in elegant free prose. It is a book that will clear the fog of doubt and vagueness — it is a book of blessing, page after page.

Sri Dayananda

19·12·04

Preface

What is the relevance of a contemplative life today? Given our single-minded pursuit of a wealth-power-success-life-style, does a spiritual life hold any attraction? Surprisingly, it does, simply because human beings are blessed with intelligence and curiosity. We have an insatiable need to know and we remain restless until we find the answers to our many questions – questions as to the reason for our dissatisfaction despite the many successes. Why are we unable to hold on to the pleasant feelings that fleet past us in succession? Where is life leading us? Where do the answers lie? Do they lie in us or in our various situations and achievements?

We know that each one of us is a self-conscious being, conscious of ourselves and the world around us. This, in turn, makes us painfully aware of our helplessness, our limitations, in relation to the world. Unable to accept this helplessness, this emptiness within us, we seek to fulfil ourselves through various experiences. The sense of satisfaction or fullness that these experiences bring, however, is either wanting or short-lived. And yet, if we can, we long to stretch these precious moments to eternity. Dedicating our lives to the pursuit of happiness, we have become endlessly seeking creatures. Chasing ever-receding goals without rest, without an end, without realising the dream of 'eternal happiness'; our lives peter out in hopeless frustration.

Is there an end to this ceaseless seeking and suffering? Not an end that comes with death, but while we are still alive? The answer, according to Vedanta, is a resounding 'Yes'. We can understand the reason if we analyse our feeling, our state of mind, when we hold what we have longed for, when we achieve the goal we have yearned for. We find we are no longer a seeking or wanting person. We the seeker, and the goal the sought, are no longer apart, separate. There is no division or split, no psychological distance between the seeker and the sought. They are one; there is neither a seeker nor a sought. We call this state of mind 'happiness', when we feel complete, full and whole.

Does this fullness come from the desired object or the goal we have achieved or does it come from ourselves, under certain conditions? The universal assumption is that the happiness lies in our achieving our goal or obtaining the object we desire. But, as we inquire further, we find there are moments when we are content without achievements, objects, persons or situations. We are faced with a possibility, no matter how incredible it appears, that perhaps the fullness lies in ourselves since we are the invariable constant in each and every achievement. If happiness were not natural to us, we would try to get rid of it the moment we feel even slightly happy. This is obviously not true since we wish to return to our happy state each and every time. When we have a headache, for example, we try to get rid of it as soon and as effectively as possible. We can conclude that headache is not our natural state. The same is true of a piece of dust in our eyes. We cannot rest until we have removed every trace of it. What is not natural to us, what is against our nature, we cannot invite, tolerate or support. Hence, we have to assume happiness is natural to us. However, our daily experiences definitely contradict this assumption. How do we resolve this apparent paradox? Could it be that we are unable to accept this hypothesis, simply because we do not know our real nature? Perhaps it is a question of self-ignorance, which means it can be resolved only by self-knowledge. This brings us naturally to the fundamental question as to the identity of ourselves, of the seeker. Who or what is

the seeker? What is his or her nature? What is his or her connection to each other and the world? This is the subject matter of Vedanta, the portion of the Vedas that deals with reality; the reality of the world, of the subject, I, the 'self'. It is the truth of the entire creation, of each one of us; in short, Vedanta is who and what we are.

Vedanta tells us that each one of us is the Limitless Whole and not helpless mortals; we are Limitless Consciousness, the cause of the world. The atma, the 'self', is the entire creation, every aspect of it; there is nothing apart from the 'self'. Equating the individual to the universal, Vedanta resolves the most fundamental of human questions, the question of god, world and man. God is not a concept in Vedanta; it is a fact, in as much as all that is here is god. God is a reality we accept, as real as the world we transact with. It further says that understanding this truth is the only way to end all sorrow and suffering and that the ending is immediate and permanent. The teaching seems to contradict all our experiences. It sounds almost audacious. Disbelief, curiosity, and hope mingled with a longing for relief, compel us to enter the teaching. One step forward and we are held spell bound by the wonder that is Vedanta, a wonder

that is firmly rooted in reality, in truth, the only unchanging fact in an ever-changing world. A greater wonder is that a master, a guru, can communicate it clearly, without doubts.

Presuming the reader has prior knowledge or, at least, an acquaintance with the basic principles of Vedanta, Without a Second cuts across the reasons for – religion, philosophy, ethics, what is Vedanta, what sets it apart from other thought processes etc. –and plunges into the heart of the subject matter with the explanation of Satyam, Jnanam, Anantam Brahma, Limitless Existence Consciousness. Using the traditional question and answer format, presented as a discussion among five persons, 'Without a Second' deals with the fundamental principles of Vedanta. Each man / woman poses questions which are answered by the protagonist, the man in grey. Since there are four persons questioning the man in grey, the topics do not always flow logically into the next. Through their various questions and answers, arguments and counter-arguments, I have presented what I have learnt and understood from the teachings of my revered master, Swami Dayananda Saraswati. The hours of constant questioning and his patient replies and explanations, how can I thank him

enough? Often, I would mull over Swamiji's words, allowing them to sink in, which they did with an ease that is nothing short of a miracle. Such a master is he that he can make his students see almost instantaneously. Swamiji's clarity of vision and his felicity of expression have combined to make him one of the greatest living masters today. His tremendous knowledge and erudition enables him to present Vedanta in a simple, yet elegant manner. He has been my inspiration, my guide in every line that I have written. I can only say 'Thank you, Swamiji. I have no words to express the deep gratitude for all that you have given me.'

Whenever Swamiji was not available, which was not infrequently, his disciple, Swamini Brahmaprakashananda Saraswati was ever willing to step in and help, withstanding my numerous questions with monumental patience. I thank her for her explanations, and most of all, her time.

Without a Second focuses on the needs of most Vedanta initiates. I hope it will help in clearing some of the doubts and commonly held misconceptions. However, an attempt to study Vedanta independently, without a master, often results in misunderstanding the texts, the words and the context. The consequent confusion and frustration may compel the student to abandon the pursuit altogether. I hope that after reading Without a Second, the reader will be sufficiently inspired to seek a teacher who can help and guide him/her on the path of self-inquiry.

Sheela Balaji
November 2004

Introduction

Without a Second, second to what, whom?
Ah! That's an interesting question
If you have the patience to listen
I shall try and explain
It all began long ago
a few wise persons discussed
the how's and why's of the world
who the creator and why the creation
why the pain and suffering
amidst the joy and laughter
tears and smiles alternating
Is there an order underlying
the seeming disorder all around
Many were the questions and doubts
they wished to discuss
thinking they would find the answers
in questioning, at first
the creator, who and where
its relation to the creation
its genius and its nature
Is there love and compassion
or is it an impassive observer

of its production
the what's and where's of the Supreme

The woman in blue said
"The One above created these
the almighty, omniscient god
He guides, seated in his glory in heaven
every little creature, every divine spark
The only purpose of our existence
to be with him, to regain our original home
worshipping him, bathed in beatific light
eternally shining like brilliant stars"

Another, "That is true in a sense
We are the same and yet different
We are a part of the One
the One with infinite divine attributes
It is the indwelling spirit, the whole
while we are the parts
inseparably locked together and yet apart"

The third stated, "Between the One and us
there is no real difference
no separation, no being a part
The One and we are not different
The differences are apparent
In essence, the One and we are the same

We could quite well say
there is no two; there is just the One
but due to our ignorance
we think that we are different"

One of the persons, as a moderator
Turned to the man in grey and said
"We know there is One
Some call it god, spirit, the 'self'
consciousness, being, true emptiness
or the all pervading absolute
What is its nature?
What is its relation to the world and us?
We are beset with conflicting opinions
separate, a part, not different
How do we know, which should we choose?
Let us hear your point of view
on this very puzzling issue"

Limitless Existence Consciousness

He was a Without a Second adherent
the man in grey, as he faced his companions
cleared his throat and began
"Before I talk of the One
Its relation to the world and us
let us inquire into the nature of the One
Our sacred books the *Upanishad*s
state in no uncertain terms
the One is Limitless Existence Consciousness
Any of these words can be used
to point to the All Pervading Absolute
not adjectives, but words in apposition
parallel words, used for the same referent
defining the essential nature of the One
Consciousness, being self – evident
It enables us to know we exist
making each one of us
self – conscious persons
with self – conscious existence
with a capacity to know, to be aware
of all that we know
all that we do not know
Every bit of information

time, space or any revelation
depends
on an already existing conscious source
for it to be known
Existence means, in essence
being, is-ness
minus subject, object or action
minus time, past, present and future
A slight movement causes a change
inviting you to ask, of any object
Which phase is? The one before?
The one present?
Or the one after the movement?
Existence has to be known
To know implies an existence
Existence can be known, only
by an existing, conscious being
a self – evident conscious source
'I know that I exist; I must exist to know'
Both Existence and Consciousness
are not different, as we can see
An example, here, may be
quite self – explanatory
When I see a book, a bird or a tree
I say, quite definitely
"A book is," "A bird is," or "A tree is"

by which I really mean
"Book consciousness is"
"Bird consciousness is"
"Tree consciousness is"
We can see
in every thought, every statement
Is-ness and Consciousness are present
Although two different words
they are not different
one includes the other
It is self – evident Consciousness
requiring no revelation
from any faculty or sense
Like a lighted candle
within the lampshade of our minds
shedding its light through our senses
It is a self – revealing conscious light
illumining our mind and senses
through them, the world
As we said earlier
the One is Existence, Consciousness, Limitless
Are these words merely adjectives?
Like a big, fragrant, yellow rose?
Separating the flower
differentiating it from many others?
'Flower' separates it

from other objects in the world
'Rose' separates it from other flowers
We can keep adding adjectives
until the particular object
is precisely pointed out
Where Existence Consciousness is concerned
these words in apposition
are words of definition
pointing to the nature of the One
They are not words of separation
since there are no 'others' to separate
no other 'existences' or other 'consciousnesses'
If doubts still arise
whether Truth is many or one
our sacred books enter
playing their inimitable role
adding, very quietly, a crucial word
'Limitless', placed in apposition
to Existence Consciousness
putting to rest all speculation
since limitless means there can be
just one
including the creation, including you and me
If a thing is 'here', it cannot be 'there'
nor can it be exactly in the same place as another
at one and the same time

There can never ever be, not even in your dreams
two limitless beings existing
because one will limit the other
Limitless means it must be
everywhere simultaneously
without a change or movement
enveloping time, space and object
Neither object nor time nor space
can limit the One, because
if they do, a conflict will result
that will surely contradict
the meaning of limitlessness
Just as water limitlessly pervades an ice cube
wood limitlessly pervades a chair or stool
we can see that limitless and all pervading
mean one and the same thing
Limitless Existence Consciousness
is the truth, the one reality
with neither parts nor particles
It is an undivided whole
in Itself, complete and full
There is never an increase
nor is there a decrease
an undivided, indivisible whole
For, if there are parts
what lies in between?

The whole will be an aggregate
a sum total of parts
making the Limitless One
dependent on its parts
There will no longer be
an all pervading being
The words Limitless All Pervading Existence
will become meaningless
Words such as 'limitless', 'all pervading'
'eternal', 'changeless existence'
each of these, point to the Limitless One
The word 'eternal' that we use
along with permanent and forever
we use it casually
in a relative sense, like ever after
What we really mean
is an extended length of time
while time and the One
have a different relation
Time places no limit on the One, it cannot
The One is the subject
while time is an object
because time has to be known
by a knowing, conscious being
There is no time the One never was
no birth, no death, no beginning, no end

no coming or going, It is, always
All Pervading, without the slightest change
You can see how illogical it sounds
when we say we will be eternally blessed
or eternally damned on a particular day
sometime in the distant future
How can we use the word 'eternal'
for an event unfolding in time?
If we are to be eternally damned
we must be damned already here and now
since eternity cannot come and go
There can be no hope for us
If we are eternally blessed
we can never be damned
since it involves the word eternal
An unthinking usage of words
resulting in much confusion
Time is the shadow of movement
A day is the earth's rotation
Splitting it results in time
of micro denominations
With further reduction
time appears as a series of moments
a series of 'now-s'
But what exactly is 'now'?
The 'now' is the present moment

Both past and future are based on it
Every past was once a present
Every future will become a present
It is from the present
we calculate both past and future
It is instantaneous, the march of moments
Even as I think of the 'now'
in a flash, it becomes the past
How can we calculate its length?
A moment, an instance
allows for millions of divisions
A division implies a length, a space
between the then and the now
between the now and the later
As we continue to divide
decreasing the length of time
time and space will merge
resulting in neither time nor space
Only the observer remains
the observer, the conscious being
who is, in essence, Consciousness
Time, space and movement
are inextricably locked together
since movement causes both time and space
Space envelops everything
Space remains unmoving

It appears to us that space
supports the entire universe
So does Consciousness
support even space
for space becomes an object
of a conscious knowing subject
The Limitless One is the basis of space
Time and space appear to bend
as do light and other elements
to suit the observer's perception
appearing as wave or a particle
depending on the mind-set of the viewer
whereas Consciousness does not bend
It is changeless existence
Change has no role in the Absolute
for changes belong to the relative world
It needs a changeless being
to give the word a meaning
Without a changeless being
what does change by itself mean?
Words such as Truth, Absolute, Being
Eternal, Real and All Pervading
each one of them refers to the One
Limitless Existence Consciousness
which is identical in essence
with I, the individual Consciousness"

"How important are these definitions?
particularly some which are so obvious"

"These words need explaining
As we go along, we will find
the explanations so germane
to the topic under discussion
Without a proper understanding
how will we know
what is real and what is not?
or the relation between the One and the world?
Without understanding the nature of the real
we cannot know the truth of ourselves and the world
It is not a point of view
It is the truth
Incredible as it may sound
it is a statement of fact
The Limitless Conscious Being
the cause of the Universe
is the same as the individual I
of the same essential nature
There being just One
the differences we see around
can only be apparent
not real as we think them"

Real (*Satyam*) and Dependent-real (*Mithya*)

"What is real and what is not
how do you decide their status?"

"Real is that which exists
without change
untouched by time or space
In this world, entropy is the rule
Change is the constant
People, emotions, objects and living things
with or without our knowing
every moment they change
How do we decide what is real? Which phase?
The nanosecond one before
or the microsecond one later?"

"The world is not real
according to you
I ask you, am I to believe
the world I experience and feel
is not real by your definition?"

"No, the world is not unreal
We can see, touch and feel

things around us
We interact with people
Feel a variety of emotions
Use various objects
to achieve our many ends
Cause and effect, ends and means
are the combinations
we use in daily transactions
In that sense, we take the world as real
But, it changes, constantly
existing within time and space
As I said before, how do I decide
on the question of its reality?
Neither is it unreal, like a leprechaun
nor non-existent, like a man
whose mother is not yet born
We have to place it
somewhere in between
Neither real nor unreal
it is difficult to categorise
this magic-like existence
It is *mithya*, dependent-real
since it draws its being
from another already existing
like a pot derives its existence
from the already existing clay

The pot is inseparable and dependent
and not 'other' than or different
from its cause the clay
The pot has no existence of its own
without the material it is made from
Dependent-real, *mithya*, is the term
Although it may appear
there are many reals
it is not true; there is only one real
Limitless Existence Consciousness
The rest, including the entire world
exist, depending on that One real
We call them *mithya*, dependent-reals
We can see, touch and use them
They have a form, name and function
relevant, in the world of transaction
They are empirically real
for they exist within a time frame
within space, limited in both ways
All that we see around us
everything in this world
our body and mind included
fall into this category
of *mithya*, dependent-reals
working within their order of reality"

Subjective Perception

"What do you mean by order of reality?
Can reality have orders and differences?"

"We have a personal subjective reality
when we perceive something
when we superimpose values
emotions, preferences and prejudices
on things which are themselves
which are just what they are
nothing less, nothing more
our individual feelings
when we respond with emotions
responses, entirely personal
to people, objects, and situations
Subjectivity plagues us
in the form of preferences and prejudices
confusing our perceptions
making us see what is not
not see what is
All through our life
our values and emotions
make our decision
but values change, for example

the time we used to play with marbles
as a child, treasuring them as precious
Then age and cynicism played their cards
we got over the craze for the coloured balls
We wonder what we ever saw
in those simple pieces of glass
If we take a rose for instance
some people love this flower
some others quite indifferent
while there are some
who could violently dislike
fragrant colourful objects
But a rose it is, just as it was made
with neither preference nor prejudice
When we mistake an object
for another that is not present
errors, illusions and delusions
including the reality of a dream
come under this category
of subjective reality
When in dull twilight
we see a piece of rope and jump in fright
thinking it is a snake, a coiled serpent
The fear leaves when we realise
it was just a rope, nothing more
Knowledge released us from the hoax

Yet while it lasted
the fear was real, wasn't it?
Another personal perception
our individual dreams
a world of our making
where dream hunger is appeased
with only dream food
The hunger in our dream
was so very real
when, we wake up and find
it was all a dream, nothing more
Just as you understand
the realness of the dream world
once you are awake
you will know what is real and what is not
when knowledge dawns and takes over
It will help you understand and see
the reality of the world and its appeal
that it is a dependent-real
depending on the All Pervading One
There is no mixing up of worlds
the world of dream and the world awake
While you were hungry in your dream
food by your bedside could not satisfy
the hunger of your dream world
Each order works within itself

Illumining the different states
enveloping them like space
is the One, the All-Pervading One
because of which exist the other levels
They belong to a different order
the order of dependent-reals"

"What about the world?
What is its order of reality?"

"The reality of the everyday world
that we perceive, with relative objectivity
perceived by the rest of the world
a world we transact with
a world of change
existing within time and space
it is an empirical reality
As we said before
these orders are *mithya*, dependent-reals
depending on the All Pervading Consciousness
from which they derive their existence
We refer to the Limitless One
as the transcendent real
since it transcends the two orders
the subjective and empirical"

"What does transcendent really mean?
Is it something beyond the world?"

"The word transcendent
means surpassing all else
something magnificent, unparalleled
How can there be more than one transcendent?
We use it for the *satyam*, the real
because the Limitless One appears as the many
lending existence to all that is here
the entire creation
while It remains untouched
without a change in Itself
Just as water is the content of all water forms
but water by itself transcends them
just as clay is the content of all clay forms
but clay by itself transcends them
and numerous other examples
Transcendent real is the only real
the rest are dependent-reals
belonging to the subjective and empirical
orders of reality"

Orders of Reality

"When you talk of orders of reality
where is the question of One?"

    "Yes, the term 'orders'
may cause some confusion
giving an existence, a reality
to what is a dependent
There is only one real
which is Limitless Consciousness
whereas the personal and transactional
levels of perception
they are *mithya*, dependent reals
A difference between the two
subjective and empirical orders
once you realised the truth
the snake disappeared
as your dreams do when you wake up
although they may leave behind traces
emotional memories of their presence
In the case of the world
it does not disappear
It continues to exist
but you will know it for what it is

just as the pot continues to exist
despite our understanding
its dependent-real status
The creation is like a dream
of the All Pervading Supreme
Its unfathomable projection
within which we, Its creations,
a picture within a picture
on a television screen
create our own special dreams
unaware and ignorant
of the reality of our being
dependent-reals, *mithya*
depending on the One All Pervading
the Limitless Consciousness"

Self Conscious Being, the Knower

"Do you mean to say
we have no independent being?
Neither my mind nor body
has any real feeling?
Am I just an illusion?
imagining a real existence?"

"We are neither illusions
nor unreal appearances
We are empirically real in an empirical world
We are conscious beings
We are alive and we know it
Each one of us know we exist
We do not need another person
to tell us we are alive or human
But we do not know our true nature
the nature of our 'self'
that we are Consciousness
with an addition of forms and names
I know 'I am', it is evident to me
It is a self-conscious, self-evident existence
We are self-conscious beings
because of the self-evident Consciousness

Just as fire heats a piece of iron
pervading every metal part
lending its essential nature of heat and light
making a cold metal appear hot and bright
Consciousness does the same
imbuing the mind and the world
enveloping the entire universe
with Its conscious presence
Just as without fire
the metal stays 'silent'
without Consciousness
to imbue us with self-consciousness
we will remain insentient
with no possibility of knowledge
not even of our existence
The Consciousness of our existence
the self-evident I, the I-Am-ness
is expressed through the mind
as the individual I
This is the locus, the base
where knowledge takes place
If I do not know that I exist, that I am
I cannot know anything
neither the world nor myself
neither what is nor what is not
In short, there will be just a void

a total darkness, emptiness
Although, even to know this blankness
we need a self-conscious existence
What is more, this debate would not exist
There will be nothing to discuss
no one to argue with
It is only because we know we are
the world, the universe, we can be aware of
Using our five senses
within our minds we perceive
the world and its dualities
of thinker and thought, seer and seen
knower and known, doer and deed
An entire universe we carry
in the inner realms of our mind
which transforms to correspond
to an object or a person
or an emotion in the external world
Recognising this mental frame, this thought-form
is what we call, cognition
The knower using the memory
identifies the thought form
the mind has assumed
"This is a chair, a flute" and so on
A problem arises however
when we, the knower

identify ourselves with the cognition
particularly if it's a mood or emotion
We think we are the state of feeling
We declare, "Oh, I am sad"
"I am depressed" or "I am glad"
It is just a thought, a mind form
never the subject, it is an object
mithya, dependent real
In fact, what we call a mind
is a bundle of thoughts
thoughts reflecting various situations
Emotions, questions and doubts
vacillating, to act or not
the 'mind' aspect at work
Second aspect, reason and logic
deciding, analysing and objective
The intellect reins in the mind
Greater its role, greater the maturity
Wisdom depends on the intellect
Third, the store of memory
unconscious' seedbed
recording each and every thought
gathered over life times
latent, character forming source
Fourth aspect covers the three
identifying thought

> forming particulars out of a whole
> first sprout of an individual
> the ego, I the singular person
> Together, the four aspects
> form the psychological part
> the subtle body of a person
> We do not recognise the truth
> that every thought and every mind-form
> is *mithya*, a dependent real
> depending on the I-Am-ness
> on the Limitless One
> the All Pervading Consciousness
> the truth of our 'self', I"

"Although it is not,
you make it sound so simple
What do you really mean by knower?"

> "Consciousness illumines the mind
> Its reflection on the mind-screen
> imbuing it with I-Am-ness
> We call it the I sense, the I thought
> which, identified with a mental frame
> assumes the role of a knower
> It is of course a relative term
> a knower in relation to the known

a thinker in terms of a thought
The knower is the subject, the I
The rest, objects, the not-I's
By a process of negation
we can sort out and remove
the I and the infinite not-I's
subject and the many objects
An exercise to understand
that what we objectify
is not I, the subject, the conscious person
just as we are not the table, the chair
nor any object or person
any situation or emotion
If we take the body
We can see it as something apart
"My body, my leg, my hand or heart"
If the leg breaks, we do not say 'I am broken'
It is the same with the rest of the organs
including our physiological system
There is no confusion
If we take the mind
our subtle internal machine
we are aware of our thoughts and emotions
If we pause to 'look' at them
they really are not us, are they?
Yet identifying with them is our habit

Our body, breath, mind and intellect
physical, physiological, psychological
aspects of a person
although we take them to be ourselves
they are objects
of a conscious being, the subject
They are dependent-reals
The world and all we see
fall into this ontological category
including the physical body
the emotions and the thoughts
Continuing with the negation, until
the mind falls silent
leaving behind the knower
alert and aware every moment
of our thoughts and actions
All these are objects
while the knower is the subject
It is the I thought
identified with a mental frame
It is the All Pervading Consciousness
appearing in the mind
as the individual I"

"What is the role of the knower
while we sleep and dream?"

"While awake, the knower is quite alert
alive to use every faculty and sense
Dreaming, the knower plays a part
in the theatre of the mind
neither awake nor asleep
passive observer of an in-between state
a world of our own
a world of replayed memories
without free-will or deliberation
It is a world of vivid imagination
curious beings, bizarre situations
so very real, we are often startled
by the dream world created by ourselves
A miracle of the Limitless One and Its *maya* force
providing a wondrous means to release
our many psychological pressures
Asleep, the knower aspect resolves
into its real nature that is Consciousness
with neither subject nor object
nor an awakened mind
a subtle mental state, luminous
like a minimised programme
on a computer screen
Hence, when we wake up, refreshed
we say, "I slept well, I can't remember
anything, not a dream, not a whisper"

Yet we are happy, despite no memory
without being aware of the world
with all the differences resolved
differences that make us limited
wanting, needing persons
Through waking and dreaming
the knower is the witness
while at sleep, it resolves into Consciousness
The knower is aware of each thought and action
aware also of their absence
but is untouched by any of them
A vital aspect, the knower
is the one real subject
without whom there can be no knowledge
Understanding the knower's nature
we can understand the truth
of our 'self' and the world
The knower essentially is not different
from the Limitless One
the All Pervading Consciousness
Consciousness is not a fourth state of experience
beyond the three
of waking, dream and sleep
It is the ultimate reality
The only one there is
basis of our existence

source of all creation
of all that is here
both known and unknown"

Individual I and Universal Consciousness An equation

"I cannot see a connection
between I, the knower, the individual
and the universal Consciousness
What is the relation?"

> "The knower, shorn of body and mind
> of the status and action of knowing
> which we call the I
> is Consciousness or Awareness
> The Limitless One, of course, is the same
> In essence, both are Consciousness
> What is different is just the name
> the form, the outer cover
> that includes the mind
> bodies of every kind
> These are *mithya*, dependent-reals"

"The One is all powerful
the creator of this universe
We are just petty mortals
Am I to believe that I am god?
How can you equate the two?"

"What we call god
is the Limitless One with Its *maya* power
To explain the essential identity
despite the obvious differences
between god and ourselves
let us look at a mathematical equation
ten minus one and four plus five
The apparent difference
may baffle a child
until the teacher explains
that despite the different numbers
the answer is the same
just as the Limitless One and I
despite the apparent differences
are not separate, different entities
They are the same
Like *this* wave and *that* ocean
their forms are many and diverse
their power, expanse and size
but their content is not different
both are water in essence
Wave-ness comes and goes
as does the ocean-ness
These are incidental qualities
not intrinsic to water
for water has no particular form

Forms are *mithya*, dependent-reals
deriving their existence from water
The wave and the ocean
are born of water, sustained by water
Finally, they resolve into water
Water is the truth, the one real
The differences are dependent-reals
The same is true of god and I, the 'self'
God-ness and the I-ness
are *mithya*, dependent-reals
If you recall your reaction
when, yesterday
I introduced you to Compassion
a man you knew some twenty years ago
You did not recognise him, you did not know
I said, "This is that Compassion
Your friend of long ago"
You were surprised
at his changed appearance
different in every way
his face, his saffron robes
The same man except, a different time
different place and a different form
but Compassion he was, just as before
This and That, those adjectival terms
brought no difference to the man

His external appearance had changed
Compassion, however, he remains
This is true of god and us
The omniscient, omnipresent, all powerful One
is the same as the mortal person, I
not in outward form or mental content
essentially both I and god, the omnipotent
are Limitless Existence Consciousness
Omnipotence and omniscience are words we use
when we speak of the Limitless One
together with Its *maya* power
in relation to the world, Its creation
Without the creation, in a resolved state
the Limitless One has no attributes
neither omniscience nor omnipotence
It is Limitless Existence Consciousness
Space provides another example
The one all pervasive expanse
contained in different vessels
appears in a variety of shapes
pots and cups, rooms and halls
but the space within these
is not different at all
Containers may change, as do sizes and shapes
The air also can vary, with the pollution of today
The space, however, remains unchanged

It is one vast expanse, one space
Space is indivisible, whole
It does not change
Nor does the Limitless One
whose nature is Consciousness
as is the I, so we must acknowledge
that between the two, there is no difference
As for proof, it is as I said before
It is back to our sacred books, the *Upanishads*
They unfailingly tell us, time and again
the All-Pervading Eternal One
together with Its *maya* power
is the same as I, the individual being
In essence, we are Limitless Consciousness
that gives existence to our ideas and situations
bringing light to the entire universe"

"Why do you relate yourself to god?
Why not to Limitless Consciousness?
Since your explanations constantly reduces
every thing we see to the All Pervading Existence"

"How can we relate to Consciousness?
It is our very nature
a fact to be understood
Besides, a relationship can exist

only within the same reality order
We cannot mix
different ontological levels
An equation exists
only between two apparent differences
as between ten minus one and five plus four
Whereas to state that water is water or five is five
are not equations; they are factual statements
As explained before
There is only one, *satyam*, real
The rest are *mithya*, dependent-reals
Just as dream food relates to dream hunger
mithya appearances relate to each other
If we look at wave and ocean
wave-ness and ocean-ness
are incidental qualities
deriving their existence from water
Water is the real
wave-ness and ocean-ness dependent-reals
Wave can relate only to the ocean
the ocean to the wave
In essence, both are water
with apparent differences
which are *mithya*, dependent-reals
Just as water is the content, the truth
of both the ocean and the wave

Limitless Consciousness is the content, the truth
Of god and the individual 'self'
Once we understand
god-ness, individual-ness, like all other 'nesses'
are *mithya*, dependent-reals
deriving their existence
from the Truth, from Limitless Consciousness
It will be obvious
that while we are Consciousness
we are related to god
the Limitless Consciousness with Its *maya* power
This is what makes us understand
we are the whole, the entire creation
bringing with it total love, total compassion
Understanding the equation
the oneness between the two
between god and the individual
is realisation, enlightenment and wisdom"

The Need for Sacred Texts

"If we are equal to the Limitless One
why do we need the sacred books?
A knower by definition
has a capacity to know
Can he or she not come to know
on his or her own
who or what the knower is?"

"To know, there must be
an already existing conscious being
the subject, the knower
How can this knower know
who or what he or she is?
He or she will need another knower
leading to infinite regression
which means no knowledge is possible
since, without a knower
knowledge cannot be established
But our experience proves
the knower exists
I know I see you; you know you see me
It is knowledge, an established fact
Infinite regression therefore

we cannot accept
With the knower's presence established
how does the knower know himself?
The knower obviously will need
help from an external source
Consciousness is never an object
It is the one real subject
Formless as It is
neither our mind nor our senses
can objectify the One Consciousness
Just as the eye cannot see itself
It needs a mirror; as does the knower
requiring an external means, a mirror
to reflect the knower's nature
This is where words play a part
words from books, words of a master
our valid means to know
this one true knowledge
knowing which everything else
is as well known
Our sacred books, the *Upanishads*
are indispensable
to reveal the knower's essence
as the One Universal Consciousness
the cause of the entire creation"

"These books were written by people like us
Why do we need them, what is their status
as the arbiter of these subtle issues?"

"Our sacred books and texts
a compendium of knowledge
equal to no other
holding within, in their deep recess
the truth of the world and us
The words reflected through the wisest of minds
their identities are lost in the mists of time
Without identity there is no impeding ego
neither subjectivity nor interpretation
Thus the knowledge has flowed
chaste
untouched by the vagaries
of individual minds
Our *Upanishads* are
revelations and not interpretations
They reveal the eternal truth
the truth of our 'self'"

Validity of the Sacred Texts

"The books describe in great detail
esoteric rites and rituals
belonging to the relative world
How can I accept such books
as the final proof
on matters of the Absolute?"

"The books are catalogues
of various human ends and means
a large supermarket of goals
of desires, must-haves and more
presenting us with choices
so numerous, we are confused
Depending on our values
our individual wisdom and preferences
we can choose from the list
enumerated in our sacred books
When they reveal or describe
a rite, ritual or even sacrifice
that guarantees future results
heavenly experience or earthly pleasures
we have no means to prove or disprove
neither accept nor reject

the revelation held in the *Upanishads*
If I have no desire
for heavenly pleasures
nor for other material gains
well aware of their transient nature
these rites and rituals
become meaningless to me
If, however, I have set my eyes
on the one true end
that helps me know for certain
the truth of my being
resolving forever my pain and sorrow
without a choice
without a second source to know
it is to the same books I must turn
to the final chapters of the texts
whose words reveal who I am
Unconcerned with the literary criticism
of constant repetition
they repeat at every opportunity
I am the One and the One is I
the cause, the source of creation
When these words are handled
by a master who knows the truth
of himself, of god and the world

they reveal without a doubt
the reality of our being
I cannot over emphasise
the sacred books' status, their importance
as valid means of knowledge
for revealing a fact that already exists
If I am not aware of a fact
that already exists, already with me
how will I ever discover it?
Particularly when the truth is I
the self-same I, the seeker of the truth?
We cannot stumble upon this knowledge
It is not a question of chance
We have to be taught, to make us understand
Just as when we look for our specs
the ones we often perch on our heads
"Where are my specs, they can't be found"
until someone says, "Look, they are on your head"
The knowledge is immediate
without lapse of time or distance
A common everyday occurrence
to find an object that is already with us
for which we needed external words
knowledge from an external source
to know we had always had them

that we never really lost them
Without words and books
we have no other means to know or find
to know that what we seek
is what we already have
What we seek to become
is what we already are
With or without our knowledge
the seeker is always the sought
Yet, we did not know due to our ignorance
Who or what can remove this not-knowing-ness?
Definitely not my mind or senses
It has to come from without
through understanding
the words from an external source
resulting in immediate knowledge
The sacred texts play this part
as a means of knowledge
by declaring the identity
of the Limitless One and the individual I
which appear at the outset
as an obvious disparity
The subject matter of the texts
is not just of the Limitless One
It reveals the nature of the I

resolving the equation
by a fundamental reduction
proving that the I
is Limitless Consciousness"

The Sacred Texts are Valid means of Knowledge

"What makes the books sacrosanct
that you quote them repeatedly?
I do not need others' opinions
to influence my thinking
It would be intellectual laziness
to accept second hand opinions
without finding out for myself
the reality of the world"

"The books are sacrosanct
because they are valid means of knowledge
particularly in matters of Truth understanding
To know
we require a valid means of knowing
means that reveal or make me know
something that is useful
that cannot be contradicted
nor countermanded nor negated
by other means of knowledge
Each of these conditions
has to be met, with precision
before we can give it the status

of a valid means of knowledge
The famous five, our indispensable quintet
ears, nose, eyes, tongue and touch
our direct means of perception
granted as part of creation's order
stream out to gather information
of objects, persons and emotions
of events and situations
storing them in our memory
Our mind taps the memory source
Expands its scope
using other means of knowledge
inference and illustration
comparison and knowledge of absence
Moving further, we have words
words from people, words from books
adding to our store of knowledge
Although, it is finally the mind
through the senses
that absorbs the knowledge gathered
In the realm of direct perception
we believe what the senses present
without a murmur of doubt
Each sense organ, like members of a band
play within their spheres, without interference
in harmony and unison

to create the music of knowledge
What our eyes tell us
our ears cannot replicate
nor what our nose brings us
can our skin duplicate
Our five sense organs
conform to the definition
of a valid means of knowledge
Our experience shows
the more means of knowledge we use
the better is our understanding
You can choose to operate
a particular means of knowledge
but once the choice is made
then the means take over
If there is an object nearby
you have good eyesight
your mind quite alert, right behind the eye
there is of course adequate light
you have no choice, no option
you will see the object
The other sense organs are no different
Once you choose to use them
you have to experience what they reveal
If you walk past a tannery
breathing quite normally

can you really deny
you cannot smell
the fetid air around?
Since despite holding your nose
the odour somehow seeps through?
It is no different with knowledge
The particular organ, the mind
must be well-prepared, disciplined
ready to absorb and understand
the subject matter of your choice
Once you have chosen to know
your wish has no role or control
over the means of knowledge
As you listen to the masters' words
knowledge will take place
If you try, you will certainly find
it works, each and every time
Our books and sacred texts are the same
When they reveal something
within our scope of understanding
we have no choice but to comprehend
the content, the truth of the words
When we come to the mind
like the others, it is also an object
of a conscious knowing subject
expressed as the knower, the I

An object cannot know the subject
Much less can an object of our senses
know their sensors
Can a flavour know the olfactory nerve?
Or a pretty picture see the eye?
Can either know the conscious director
The knower aspect of the mind?
Effects cannot reverse the flow of knowledge
The mind and senses are effects
They cannot know the one who directs
the knower, the subject, the I
How will we know who or what the knower is?
We can never know on our own
We need the words of our sacred books
to reveal the truth of the I
that it is not different from the Limitless One
the cause of the creation
Our mind and senses cannot countermand
the words of our sacred books
since what the words reveal
does not oppose or negate
the essence of our mind and senses
nor does the truth lie within the scope
within the purview of our mind and senses
How can these contradict
the truth of our sacred books?"

Beyond the Senses and Mind

"If It is beyond our senses and our mind
how will we find the truth of the One?
It stands to reason
the Limitless One is beyond us"

    "Beyond our mind and senses
    a phrase to emphasise
    it is not an object of our mind
    The One Limitless Consciousness
    has neither form nor figure
    no attributes or qualities
    How can the mind and senses objectify It?
    We cannot know the Limitless One
    as we know an object
    It is *the* truth of our 'self'
    The Limitless One illumines the mind
    making it sentient
    It is the eye of the eye
    the one real subject
    the mind and senses, objects
    The One is, as it were, the cause
    My mind, the effect, a dependent-real
    How can a dependent-real know

the Consciousness that makes it known?
Hence, we call it beyond the mind"

"It is often said in our sacred books
the old masters taught the truth
in silence, they had no need for words
since words are inadequate
to convey the Absolute
Perhaps, this is what is meant
by beyond our senses?"

"How can you teach in silence?
If the masters respond with silence
to each and every question
the student will interpret
the silence, differently
colouring the silence
with a personal overtone
If, in response to a question
on the existence of a creator
the master remains silent
each student may conclude
'There is no creator
Yes, there is a creator
but he cannot be described
The master wants us to find out

on our own, he likes independence'
Infinite other interpretations
of the master's silence
How will the students find
the answers to their questions?
With neither teachers nor teaching
neither words nor means of communicating
the truth of the Absolute
there will be no end to our seeking
no end to our life of suffering
This cannot be
since the relative world
consists of pairs of opposites
One does not exist without the other
No darkness without light
nor sorrow without joy
or problems without solutions
That is the order of the creation
If no solution or answer exists
to our endless search
creation would be defective
But it is not so; order is the norm
Our seeking implies a sought
Words are second to none
in communicating the vision
through means that are known

since we cannot communicate
an unknown through another unknown
Words and their meanings are known
The masters use them to reveal the truth
Since the Limitless One has no form
no qualities or attributes
words cannot reveal directly
the nature of the All Pervading One
Silence means
revealing indirectly
by implication, using words in apposition
pointing out subtly, but clearly
with absolute certainty
words wielded by a master
who can reveal with clarity
the vision of our *Upanishads*
The truth of the All Pervading Being
is the truth of the knower, of the I
This is what we mean by 'teaching in silence'
It is neither mystic nor esoteric
to open itself to interpretation"

Many Texts and Interpretations

"How are you so certain
of the books in your tradition?
In your particular interpretation?
There are many versions
other books in the world
What is the basis to consider
your books, your views to be the superior?"

"Of course, others proclaim aloud
their texts are the true revealed words
In this, we have to judge the books
by scrutinising their contents
Are there no discrepancies, no contradictions
stating one thing first and denying them later?
Do they stand to logic, reason and experience?
Is there immediacy, a here and now
not after death accounts
in the knowledge held in their books?
Knowledge to be understood
not a matter of faith, fantasy or belief?
Do they reveal the true nature of our 'self'
god the omnipotent one and I are the same
Limitless Existence Consciousness

the basis of all existence?
Knowledge that reiterates time and again
we are already, here and now, the Limitless whole?
Knowledge that sets us free, immediately
from the wrong notion that we are limited beings?
Knowledge, I cannot know on my own?
Knowledge that cannot be improved upon?
Which can be communicated clearly, without doubts
With a methodology to make any academician proud?
If we consider these questions
you can see for yourself
our sacred texts and commentaries
speak for themselves
What's more, I must add
if we look at the books, objectively
they declare equivocally
that truth is Without a Second
the Limitless One and I are not different
the One is I, that is, Consciousness
source of all creation
So the point 'Without a Second'
is definitely the right conclusion
It is the truth
The Limitless One and I are one"

"If I understand you rightly,
no other interpretation
than Without a Second
is at all possible
Yours is the last word on it
the rest is mere ignorance
With more people of your opinion
we will not have any more openness
a society of closed-minded persons
will be the result"

"I am not the decision maker
It is not a personal opinion
I am only pointing out
the validity of the words
of our sacred books and texts
Others' explanations merely restate
what our minds and senses tell us
the world and we are different
Some of our most reputed teachers
masters and preachers
have fallen into this subtle trap
of using the sacred words and texts
to support their interpretations
However well meaning they may have been
the fact remains they have not been

quite as objective as they claim to be
They have superimposed on the sacred words
their chosen points of view
using the texts, perhaps, unknowingly
as a vehicle for their hypotheses
I do not need to study
for twelve long years
to repeat, restate the obvious
'The world and I are different'
that would indeed be laughable
It would be like telling a child
'You know, don't you?
the horse and you, my child
are not the same?
You are different'
The child would look at me
most curiously
wondering what had happened
to its wise, almighty Papa
The same applies
to the others' explanations
Truth is not a matter of faith or belief
with every prophet making fabulous claims
How can we ever know for sure
which claim is the true one?
What is their valid source?

Without immediacy, logic or reason
how can we consider their source
as valid means of knowledge?
You will find as you learn
that Without a Second
is not a matter of opinion
It is a statement of fact
nor is it a point of view
A point of view we can have
only when we know the entire view
when we have the vision of the whole
Where the truth is concerned
to have the entire vision
we need to look at what the words tell us
without prejudice, with objectivity
Once we know the whole
Where is the need for a point of view?
Truth not seek popular appeal
nor is it a question of an opinion poll
A society that seeks the truth
by definition will be
the most open of societies
Our present debate proves
we are avid seekers of truth"

The Sacred Texts are Dependent-reals

"Your sacred texts and books
are objects, dependent-reals
Yet you call them revelations
using them as valid means of knowledge
to support your arguments
Objects as they are
belonging to the relative world
how can they speak of the Truth Absolute?"

"Yes, the books are dependent-reals
but, we are living in a world
of dependent-reals, a world of *mithya*
Our mind and body included
belong to this order of reality
As I said earlier, each order works within itself
What works in one, does not work in the other
If you are hungry in your dream
it is only dream food that will relieve
Food from our waking world
cannot, does not have a role
It is the same for the books
In a world of transaction, a relative world
a dependent existence, a dependent-real

relative knowledge alone
can remove relative ignorance
Our *Upanishads* and texts
belong to this relative order of reality
They help to remove the ignorance
belonging to the same relative existence
The words peel away from us
layer upon layer of not-knowing-ness
until we can clearly see
the Truth of the 'self' and the world
Thus, despite their dependent status
our books help us understand the Absolute"

"How do I know for certain
the words speak the truth?
I cannot blindly believe
without positive proof"

"If we listen to what the words reveal
with an alert mind, with total objectivity
allowing the words to speak for themselves
the very same texts will bless us
with the vision of the truth
We will see it works every time
by releasing us instantly
from all limitations and fears

If, for instance, an ophthalmologist
after a long surgery says
"You can see if you open your eyes"
The patient, ever suspicious, replies
"Promise me I can see
only then will I open my eyes"
He does not give the surgeon a chance
He has neither faith nor trust
Without positive proof he cannot believe
the surgeon's words
When the books talk of the Absolute
they can and do work
If we enter them, impartially
aware of our limited mental capacity
willing to listen to the words
with faith and humility
taking them to be
valid means of knowing
they reveal not directly
but by implication
the truth of the One and the I
Limitless Existence Consciousness
cause of the universe"

"If you consider the sacred books
as revealed texts and revelations

What about our thoughts?
After all, according to your opinion
Consciousness illumines the mind
The mind gives birth to thought
Hence every thought is illumined
by the One Consciousness
It is a revelation
If that is true
how will you explain the violence
that we see in the world?
the cruelty, the hurt, people inflict?"

"A revelation is an idea, a thought
revealing something unknown
something useful
unavailable for independent knowing
If we are to use them
as a means of knowledge
they must also conform to the definition
of a valid means of knowing
They must not be contradicted
or countermanded by other means of knowledge
They must be completely objective
without ego's influence
to colour them with subjective tones
Every thought therefore cannot be a revelation

Although we can definitely say
every thought is revealed
since it is Consciousness
that brings each of them to light
As for violence and hurt
they reflect the psychological order
a person's mind comes under
revealing an inner turmoil
clouding the sense of discrimination
encrusted, as it were
by hatred and anger
tendencies carried forward
from the remote or recent past
fanned into flames in the present
by a turbulent childhood
other situations that life unfolds
Again, every action has a reaction
Hatred and violence will take their toll
of the perpetrator's mind and spirit
What worse punishment can there be
than a deadening of one's sensitivity?
With no hope for relief
nor even a desire for it?
Suffering unknowingly
tormented within in great disquiet?

Violence brings its own miseries
through internal or external agencies
Cause and effect rules can never be denied
whereas the actions that harmonise
with the order we see all around
there is peace and tranquillity
a sense of well-being
of both body and spirit
a sensitive mind
concerned with others' welfare
alive to others' feelings"

Sentient and Insentient

"Since the One is Consciousness
Why do we have differences
such as sentient and insentient?
The world must have
no inanimate objects"

"We are animate beings
Yet, from our body grows
many inanimate objects
hair and nails, teeth and bones
From the inanimate earth
emanate animate beings: plants and trees
If we look at our dreams
we have both animate and inanimate objects
lakes and hills, animals and human beings
created by us, the sentient person
It is the same with Consciousness
Creating out of Itself, using Its *maya* power
the world, the universe
animate beings and inanimate objects
If we turn to science for example
the entire universe
can be reduced to particles

atomic dust
wielded by a genius
a magician par excellence
producing different objects
animate and inanimate
living and non-living
Like the power of electricity
is manifest in such diversity
fan, light, computers and TVs
Consciousness expresses Itself
in an astonishing variety
The world reflects Its capacity
Its knowledge, Its intelligence
in the laws, the orders, that we see around
physical, chemical, botanical
psychological, biological and other fields
For the world, as it were, is an assemblage
a putting together so elegantly, intelligently
that we, as conscious beings
can know, understand and learn
the workings of this wondrous creation"

"Creation imputes a motive, a desire
on the part of the creator
Does the One have a mind?"

"All-knowing definitely means
knowing without a mind
since a mind implies thinking
which is an action, a mental one
involving time and space
It would give a lie to the words
Limitless Existence Consciousness
The Limitless One together with Its *maya*
whom we call the creator
is all knowledge, always
If he thinks or acts
he is no different
From us humans
Our mind, limited by time and space
limited by its capacity
we can know only a minuscule part
and that, sequentially
We cannot process a million problems
at one and the same time, simultaneously
whereas omniscience means all knowledge, at once
There is nothing else besides, including ignorance
since knowledge of ignorance is also knowledge
Because god is all knowledge
manifest as the laws, the order that is the world
every discovery, every new learning

fills us with joy
a reflection of the joy infinite
that is the nature of the Limitless One"

Origin of Ignorance

"If the One is intelligence and knowledge
where is the place for ignorance
the cause of much confusion?
Where did it all begin?
It seems to me there are two
ignorance and knowledge"

"Ignorance has no real existence
nor is it the absence of knowledge
It is a dependent-real
Something we are aware of
existing within time and space
Our experience proves
ignorance comes with birth
As we learn, we come to know
data, facts and information
our ignorance vanishes
So, ignorance cannot be a real
It is *mithya*, a dependent-real
existing within a time frame
whereas knowledge is the One's nature
It does not come and go
nor is it relative knowledge opposing ignorance

It is knowledge in the absolute sense
It is Limitless Existence Consciousness
lighting up both knowledge and ignorance
making us aware that we know
as well as that we do not know
As for the beginning of ignorance, tell me
since when do you not know Lithuanian?"

"I have never thought of learning
such an obscure language"

"Obviously, you cannot say when
the language ignorance began
If you wish, however, you could learn
With learning
the ignorance of Lithuanian
will definitely vanish
A curious thing, ignorance
although it has no beginning
it does have an ending
What is more
once it goes, it never returns"

Cause and Effect

"If you say everything
is the All Pervading Consciousness
How do you explain the differences
that we see around us?
Such diversity of forms
an enormous variety
yet, you say there is just One?
Does the One shatter into many?"

    "In a world of clay
    a world of different forms and shapes
    each one of them is clay
    You can count the effects, the pots
    the cups and other clay objects
    How will you count the clay?
    You cannot get further than one
    Effects may come and go
    The cause alone remains
    If we look at creation
    with its infinite forms
    we would think
    diversity is the rule
    whereas the truth

is quite the opposite
Every object can be reduced
to invisible particles
so subtle that they are only inferences
thoughts in our minds
They are objects
of a conscious subject
Constantly changing and becoming
they are dependent-reals
without independent existence
What remains is the knower, the I
the one subject, the only real
which is not different
from Limitless Existence Consciousness
Using examples of cause and effect
we can arrive at the same conclusion
If we take pot and clay
or gold and chain
every part, every detail
of the pot is only clay
There is no part of the pot
where the clay is not
We could also say, could we not
that clay pervades the pot?
Where the pot is concerned
clay is the limitless one

the all pervading material
No matter which preposition we use
on or in, up or down
beside or beneath, above or below
you cannot separate
the pot from the clay
Born of clay, sustained by clay
finally, when the pot breaks
it resolves into clay
Clay alone remains, clay is the truth
where the pot is concerned
It is the real
the pot, a dependent-real
depending on its material
It has no separate existence
apart from clay, its essence
Where is the pot?
In fact, there really is no pot
There is just clay, the material
with an incidental quality of pot-ness
a quality neither intrinsic nor extrinsic
since every time I think of clay
a pot does not come to mind, right away
You can have different forms
different shapes and sizes
Every one of them is clay

Let us take another example
of gold and the many golden objects
a tonne of gold can become
a tonne of different ornaments
Each one of them
is made of gold, sustained by gold
resolves into gold
Gold is the all pervading source
of each golden object
Every part is gold
Its worth and weight the same as gold
Is a gold wedding band more precious
than the gold it is made from
because of our sentiment?
Any jeweller will refute your claim
Gold is all the value it has for him
You can count each one of the objects
a million diverse golden forms
whereas the shiny yellow gold
it is not manifold
it is one, gold
An effect cannot exist
without its cause
No matter how fertile our imagination
we cannot conceive of an uncaused effect
If we look at a shirt, for instance

can it exist without a material?
It cannot, it is not possible
The cause is the only real
The rest are effects
mithya, dependent-reals
The clay and gold, of course
require external sentience
to create the many objects
whereas, the Limitless One, the real
the cause of all causes
together with Its *maya* power
appears as the many
without another intervening
another sentient intermediary
The One without a cause
is both intelligence and matter
maker and material
It is One Limitless Existence
All Pervading around us
We can 'see' Its presence
if we truly understand
the One All-Pervading
is the same as I, the individual being
that is self-revealing, Limitless Consciousness"

Creator and Creation

"How can you be so dismissive
of the very essence of our being?
If everything is the One
how will you explain this creation?
When did it all begin?
Your postulate makes the world an illusion
something non-existent, a figment of our imagination"

"The world is neither non-existent nor an illusion
It has a form, a name and a function
But it is a dependent-real
as is the creation
Creation is not a real action
There is no real object creation
It is a manifestation
brought forth by the Limitless One
out of Itself, without the slightest change
remaining as It is
using Its power, Its energy
When we see a beautiful tapestry
we infer the existence
of a talented weaver
with both the knowledge and the skill

needed to produce the wonderful fabric
Like a crafts-person who knows
every detail of his chosen craft
with the knowledge and the talent
required to produce the chosen object
If we extend the reasoning
to the world, the creation
when we look around us
we find a world put together
with tremendous intelligence
We infer the presence
of an Intelligent Maker
with the knowledge of the universe
The Limitless One with Its *maya* power
knows the entire creation
in every detail, a total precision
of the past, present and the future
both a bird's eye view and a worm's
the reason we call It omniscient
The only problem in the examples
of the pot and the pot maker
the weaver and the fabric
the conscious person and the material
there is a division, a space between them
They are apart, the material 'becomes' another
losing its original status, its original character

But the creator and the material are not different
The All Pervading One is both creator and creation
without a change, without becoming
It is both intelligence and matter
If the two are apart
there will be a separation
a gap, a distance
creating time and space
The creator will have to move
travelling, creating, moulding
a constant changing, transforming
a world of becoming
an incessant cycle of metamorphosis
What would be the meaning
of an All-Pervading Existence?
Besides, with two separates
maker and material
each will limit the other
contradicting the words
of the *Upanishads*
"All that is here is One"
"The One is all knowledge"
"This I is the All Pervading One"
They not only declare the One is
"Limitless, Existence, Consciousness"
They go a step further

equating the individual I with the Limitless One
Hence, intelligence and matter
creator and creation must remain
with the one source, the one real
Just as a spider spins a web
drawing the silk from itself
the Limitless One draws from within
all the material needed
for the world to be created
Like your dreams, you create them
projecting them from within
resolving them when awake
You are therefore both
cause and effect
creator and the creation
where your dreams are concerned
The world, also, is an effect
while the Limitless One is the cause
Playing a double role
the self-same One
of inventor and invention
Cause and effect, however
are relative terms
Words of cause and effect need each other
to convey the meanings they were intended for
An author is an author because of his writing

A mother, a mother, in relation to her child
Minus any writing, can we call him an author?
Without a child, can she be a mother?
When the effect is *mithya*, dependent-real
constantly changing
without inherent existence
without inherent identity
ontologically a dependent-real
drawing its being
from a conscious subject
the role of the cause as a cause
definitely falls apart
It is the same with the creation
It has no real existence
mithya, dependent-real in essence
Where is the cause, the creator?
Its role as a cause negated
It remains what It always is
that is Consciousness
Seen from the world angle
from the effect's point of view
the Limitless One is the creator, the cause
while by Itself
in Its essential nature
It is neither effect nor cause
It is All Pervading Consciousness

which is not different
from I, the individual consciousness
As for your question
the where and when of creation
There is really no where and when
It is an endless cyclic manifestation
a constant resolution and projection
making manifest what was potential
while a resolution is just the opposite
The Limitless One uses Its infinite power
Its *maya*, Its cosmic force
with which It projects, sustains
resolves the entire universe
The Limitless One lends existence, It is the canvas
for this enormous cosmic illustration"

Is Creation an Action

"If like the spider, the One spins
It is no different from us
It acts, so It cannot be real
the word according to your definition"

"It is a manifestation, rather than a creation
The All Pervading One
does not change, does not work
Out of Itself, without a will or action
It brings forth the universe
Gives it a conscious existence
that is Its nature and essence
We need language to communicate
Verbs are a must
We cannot do without
The way you brought out your dreams
Which verb should I use to explain them?
While you slept, you were unaware
of your mind's mental dramatics
With no wilful action on your part
the unconscious set free
your memories had a field day
unwinding, replaying

their complicated contents
You were the base, the locus
for the dreams to be exposed
You did nothing, you just were
The same is true of the Limitless One
remaining at It is without a change in Itself
neither an increase, nor a decrease nor a metamorphosis
It is both the creator and the creation
manifest as the world
It is the screen
on which the world cinema is projected
Without the screen, there is no movie
It is the support of all that we see
For the bubbles on the ocean
the froth and waves
the ocean is their support
basis of their existence
The entire universe, a dependent-real
has its source, its very being
in the One, All Pervading"

"Why do you use the term 'without a second'?
Since you reduce everything
to a conscious subject
why not call it One?"

"It is one without a two
without a following number
If we pause to think
what the number one means
we will find it so elusive, so deceptive
because what we count as one
is in fact more than a million
If we look at a wall for instance
there is one wall, yes
but made of many bricks
If we take a single brick
it has numerous grains of sand
Each grain of sand, millions of particles
Incredible as it may sound
what we term as one
is just an appearance
a number we use
as a matter of convenience
Precisely because 'one' is a myth
in the relative world
in a world of opposites
a world of dualities
we call Truth 'Without a Second'
pervading and transcending as It is
this universe of forms and names

There is only *satyam*, the rest is *mithya*
Truth is thus neither one nor two
It is non-dual"

The World after Knowledge

"Just as ignorance disappears
with the advent of knowledge
Does the world vanish
once we have understood
the truth of the I as the One
Limitless Existence Consciousness?"

"No, it does not
If we look at particles
they offer excellent examples
Every object, every person
is a mass of atoms
But we take the form as tangible
something solid and palpable
while, in fact, they are nothing more
than invisible particles, atomic dust
Despite what science has proved to us
we continue to transact with the universe
Just as it is the earth that rotates and revolves
yet, we remark
"Look at the sun rise"
The same is true for the world appearance

We take as real, this existence
permanent and with substance
Even after we understand
its level of realness
the world will not disappear; it will exist
but it will not bind us
We will know it for what it is
a dependent-real, the entire world
an incidental quality
superimposed, projected
by our not-knowing-ness
on the One Being, Limitless Existence
the All-Pervading Consciousness
which is the same, in essence
as the knower, the I"

Projection and Superimposition

"What do you mean by a superimposition?
If we superimpose
what happens to the base?
It must surely change
Yet, you say it is incidental?"

"It is a projection of a quality
on an already existing base
like pot-ness on clay
The clay can take on any form
lid-ness, cup-ness and others
It remains untouched, unchanged
by these qualities
They are incidental, not intrinsic
If pot-ness is intrinsic to clay
we cannot have a variety of clay objects
Instead, we will have a pot
wherever there is clay
But clay exists by itself
with or without pots and cups
It is obvious that the 'nesses'
are only incidental to clay
We call them superimpositions

of forms and names
on an already existing base
If we take a flower or any other
we find it is made of many parts
but by themselves
the parts are not the flower
Sepals, petals, calyx and others
each, a non-flower in itself
Heaping them together
does not make a flower
Yet when put together intelligently
they acquire a form, name and function
appearing as the flower in question
Although it sounds a contradiction
to say non-flower makes a flower
it is the truth, *maya's* magic power
reflecting the genius of the creator
A further step, an extension
we can very well state
there is no flower
there is only an object, a 'this'
with the quality of flower-ness
superimposed on it
In every perception there exists
the knower, I, the conscious subject
the known, 'this', the object

'This' signifies proximity in time and space
of things other than I
When we perceive something
we first sense its existence
an indistinct feeling
and within an instant, clearly
We say, "This is"
The 'this' can be
table, flower or tree
people, objects and emotions
a list of the entire creation
Each one of them, we could declare
'flower is, tree is, chair is'
If we analyse these statements
'is' or existence is the common element
while the objects, they differ
What exactly are these objects?
Each object has a particular 'ness'
unique to itself
If it has tree-ness, we call it a tree
with flower-ness, a flower
an endless list of 'nesses'
qualities superimposed
on the substratum of existence
the is-ness, the 'this', that we first sense
Every 'ness' is a projection

an incidental quality
on a base which must be
without that particular 'ness'
since to project flower-ness
on an already existing flower
would definitely be meaningless
So, flower-ness on non-flower
tree-ness on non-tree
world-ness on non-world
universe-ness on non-universe
Every 'ness' on a non-'ness'
What exactly is a non-object, a non-ness?
Non-object is the same as existence
is-ness without an object
without quality or attribute
Is-ness is the same as Consciousness
because to state 'something is'
implies a conscious being
The 'nesses' are incidental qualities
How can they affect the base, the real?
Can the pot affect the clay?
Can the snake affect the rope?
Two different orders of reality
cannot connect with each other
Consciousness the real
the world a dependent-real, *mithya*

How can *satyam*, real,
connect with *mithya*, dependent-real?
We transact with the world
experience its diversity
What is its status of reality?
Being *mithya*, dependent real
the world-ness, the universe-ness
all the 'nesses'
can only be incidental qualities
superimposed on existence
If they were to be intrinsic
we would hold on
to the first object we perceive
It would be the truth, a real
It cannot change; it never will
We will continue seeing
that one first thing
all through our life
a perception we cannot leave
Thus unable to see another object
unable to perceive the diversity
life itself would be
an impossibility
Our experiences refute
such absurdities
We perceive instead

a world of diversity
Another instance to elucidate
When I perceive an object
a 'seer-ness' is imposed on me
If that 'ness' is intrinsic to me
I would be a seer forever
never a hearer or a speaker
This contradicts my experience
It is clear that all the 'nesses'
are incidental qualities
a superimposition on existence
If we assume these are intrinsic qualities
and we perceive a variety of objects
then the variety we perceive
would each be a 'real'
being intrinsic to existence
How can we understand
the words of our sacred books
statements such as "That I am"
"All that is here is the One"?
The words would stand negated
since everything will be a 'real'
with permanent existence
resulting in our being
in perpetual conflict
bound, limited and helpless

which my own daily experiences
definitely refute
When I am asleep, deeply
with no dreams to disturb me
tasting a sense of unity
how happy I am with no differences
no divisions to separate me
With what eagerness I look forward
to that dreamless state!
Obviously, the varieties that we perceive
cannot be reals
The world and the infinite 'nesses'
can only be adventitious appearances
superimposed
on Existence Consciousness"

Reality of Superimposition

"How do you call it a superimposition?
I can see it, feel it and use it
Yet, you negate it
equating it to a magic trick?"

"It is like the rope-snake
Did you not react in fear?
Sweating and shaking, was it not real?
Snake-ness you superimposed
on what was just a rope, a non-snake
The snake was purely subjective
since you were its only witness
But it did make you jump
despite it being non-existent
In that sense, it had a reality
although only for you
while the pot, a dependent-real
serves the general world
A world of transaction
with its form, name and function
allows for various relations
cause and effect, ends and means
Despite its usefulness

pot-ness, as explained before
like all the other 'nesses' of the world
is a superimposition
on Is-ness which is Consciousness
The world including my mind and body
has a definite form, name and purpose
Being *mithya*, dependent-reals
they can only be superimpositions
on Limitless Existence Consciousness"

The Cause of Projection

"Why do we project?
What is the cause
of the many superimpositions?"

"Partial knowledge and partial ignorance
they are the causes
for our mistakes, our projections
If there is total ignorance
no projection is possible
When you know a certain something is
you do not know exactly what it is
This is the point where error occurs
The 'something' is the base
for projections to take place
The rope was the base
the snake, a projection
If we look at ourselves
unwittingly, we commit this mistake
the fatal flaw that binds us
to the never ending loop of life
From total freedom to bondage
from light into darkness
is just a step away from knowledge

into a world of not-knowing-ness
We are ignorant of our ignorance
We do not know
who or what we are
I know that I am, that I exist
that I am a conscious being
I do not know
I am the Limitless Consciousness
identifying instead
with my psycho-physical self
I am the body and mind
the body and mind is I
Misapprehension of all people
taking the subject as the object
the object as the subject
thereby limiting the Limitless
The real as the dependent
the same in reverse
a potent mixture
of knowledge and ignorance
the cause of all projections
You can replace the word 'body'
with any other word
labelling ourselves
to suit body, mind or status
Fat, thin, tall or short

happy, sad, angry or calm
successful, a failure, an also ran
it would be a false identity
Maya's two-fold power is at work
veiling the truth and projecting the world
Mesmerised by its magic
we take the world to be real
until serendipitously we come across
a sage, a master, who opens our eyes
to what is real and what is not"

Maya's Veiling Power

"Who superimposes or projects?
With what?"

"No one superimposes; it is not an action
placing an object on another
or transferring a picture
Due to beginning-less ignorance
our minds befuddled by *maya's* presence
confuses our understanding
of the reality of things
Maya's presence prevents us
from knowing things in their completeness
A table for instance
we do not know its molecular structure
or the many laws that govern it
nor the how's and why's of its making
If we view one angle, we cannot see the others
at one and the same time
This is true of the other objects
including people and personal relations
Unaware of the world's real-ness
we think that what we see
is an absolute reality

When we saw a rope
we thought it was a snake
We reacted accordingly
As in our dreams
we believe the reality
of our make-believe world
Unknowing of the truth
Limitless Existence Consciousness
is the truth of our 'self'
we accept the world and everything we see
the differences and the diversity
as the one real, the only real
thinking we are forever bound
with no hope of relief
from our worries and care
until we drop our bodies
leaving our earthly existence
Whereas when the truth is understood
we will know the reality of the world
freeing us forever, instantaneously
from the sense of bondage"

"How can there be a superimposition
without someone to superimpose?
If it is *maya*, how does it act?"

"With its power of ignorance
that comes along
with our first breath
The moment we are born
in our mind appears
a reflection of the Limitless One
the I-Am-ness, the I sense
which instantaneously identifies
with the body and mind
results in a self-conscious being
the individual I
No matter how rudimentary the species
it is imbued
with the primal desire to survive
Visible in every form of life
Using the mind and senses
it incites the body to act
to keep the organism alive
Caught in a spiral
the I continues
propelled by its actions
its sense of doer-ship
owning up its deeds
through infinite life times
repeating endlessly
the circle of life

Truth of the I masked
maya's magic at work
Unknowing
of our Limitless nature
a new world begins
a creation of sorts
a world of our making
a world of separation
I, me, mine, you, he, she, it and so on
So unshakeable is our belief
in the reality of the world
such confidence we repose
on our minds and senses
we cannot accept
the dependent-reality of the world
including our mind and body
Maya's double act, its twin roles at play
one of keeping us ignorant
of the truth of ourselves
another of leading us to believe
in the reality of the projected world
The two aspects of ignorance
veiling and projecting
working in tandem
cause of our confusion, of our superimposition
In our dreams

only when we are 'dead' to the waking world
can we enter the world of dreams
We cannot be in both
simultaneously
One disappears while the other appears
Understanding the truth is different
Despite the knowledge of the world's reality
the world does not disappear
nor does our body and mind
We continue to transact
living and working in the world
using the infinite forms and names
knowing they are *maya's* games"

Maya's Ontological Status

"Who or what is *maya*?
What is its status of reality?"

"We need not say if *maya* exists or not
A single word cannot capture
the reality of *maya*
Neither existing nor non-existent
neither real nor unreal
a curious ontological phenomenon
it does not sustain analysis
constantly changing
depending on the One Limitless
for its existence
It is bound by time and space
appears for the moment to be real
with a form, a name and function
We can use it for transaction
Yet we cannot categorically state
it really exists
This is the mystery of *maya*
Since it derives its existence
from a conscious being
it is *mithya*, dependent-real
This is *maya's* ontological status"

Maya and the Limitless One – What is the Connection

"By presenting two, separate beings
the Limitless One and *maya*
you have negated the essence
of Without a Second"

"The Limitless One and *maya*
are like a person and his power
his strength and his energy
He can use and wield these
either reveal or resolve them
in any manner he chooses
They are not separate entities
There is only one, the conscious being
with power and energy resting on him
How can they exist independently?
They are dependent-reals, *mithya*
depending on a conscious being
Although the subject can be
minus the energy
the energy cannot be
without a sentient subject
Maya, inseparable and dependent

the energy force of the Limitless One
depends on the One Consciousness
It does not exist by itself, it cannot
It has no real existence
It is *mithya*, a dependent-real
It is the source of all dependent-reals
that is the entire creation
It is the One's energy-material
with which the Limitless One
manifests Itself as the universe
without Itself changing
Seen from the world angle
the Limitless One is at once
both the intelligent and the material source
of the entire universe
Just as the pot is neither separate
nor is it a part of clay
the pot is clay
the world is neither separate
nor a part of the Limitless One
The world IS the Limitless One
with an addition of forms and names
with an addition of attributes
There is no question of two
There is just the One
Limitless Existence Consciousness"

"What is the connection
between the One with no attributes
and the world full of attributes?"

"There is no real connection
since the world is *mithya*, dependent-real
as is its source, *maya*, the cosmic force
the power of the Limitless One
How can *mithya* connect with *satyam*, the truth?
If we mistook an oyster shell
for a silver object
did the metal really exist?
Although the rope-snake frightened us
did the snake really exist?
Silver and snake are *mithya*
How can they affect the real?
Two different ontological levels
cannot connect with each other
Where the world is concerned
it is *mithya*, a dependent-real
constantly changing
existing within time and space
dependent on *satyam*, real
The connection between the two
real and dependent-real
is neither cause and effect

nor one of ends and means
It is a superimposition
of forms and names
on the Limitless One
a superimposition caused by our ignorance
of what is real and what is not
We take the pot to be real
when it is but a dependent-real
In a world of clay
it is clay that is the real
the forms and names, an addition
dependent-reals
Born of clay, sustained by clay
they are only clay
with a superimposition of pot-ness
lid-ness, cup-ness
a host of other 'nesses'
The world-ness is similarly
mithya, dependent-real
It is form, name and function
superimposed on the Limitless One
When we inquire into its reality
we find it has no real substance
It exists within time and space
with change as its constant
depending on Truth for its existence

Truth that is Limitless Consciousness
Our ignorance caused by *maya's* presence
causes our misapprehension
results in our not knowing
what is real and what is not
Maya's raison d'etre explains
the apparent existence of the world
its apparent connection to the Limitless One
Like the eighteenth elephant*
that vanishes after serving its purpose
once we understand the truth
maya's presence no longer confuses us
Seen from the creation's point
maya is the power, the material
with which the Limitless One manifests Itself
Once *maya's* reality is understood
we can see clearly
its dependent-reality
that it is energy and matter
dependent on and inseparable
from the Limitless One
It is not a separate entity
Where is the question of a connection?
There is only one existent
which is Limitless Consciousness
the source of the universe"

"How does *maya* become the world?
Dependent-real that it is
does it have the capacity to reveal
the Limitless One's intelligence?"

"Just as in the hands of a skilful potter
the humble clay, despite its insentience
reveals the potter's skill and talent
appearing as beautiful clay objects
maya is the cosmic material
universal energy-matter
capable of revealing
the genius that is the Limitless One
An example from our *Upanishads*
provides an illustration
of a spider drawing silk
from within, without a change in itself
It is both the maker and the material
but it is the spider that weaves
not the silk
insentient material that it is
It is no different with *maya*
It cannot create
It is the Limitless One that manifests
drawing the material from Itself
It is both the maker and the material

of the manifest universe
At first, neither time nor space
just the One pregnant with creative force
A breathless moment
expands like ethereal mist
Maya's presence now palpable
crystallising into a world
as time the shadow of space enters
Out of the Limitless One, without an action
streams *maya* of three kinds
rolled into one, a triple effect
A calm peaceful one, clear and perfect
Another more energetic, powerful and frenetic
The third is like a resting state
resembling sleep, to recuperate
From the three now emanate
subtler than the subtlest
space, wind, fire, water, earth
Maya in infinite combination forms
the nature, trait and character
of the various kinds of persons and matter
It is the creative material
the fundamental energy matter
building block of the universe
issuing forth from the Limitless One
The creator's knowledge

when manifest through matter
Consciousness expressed
we recognise Its presence
Every object in the world
assembled for a purpose
for us to marvel and wonder
implies a genius in its creation
particles put together
to appear as the object in question
Every part of the object
reveals the intelligence of its maker
in the laws, the orders
in the formation, the structure
a perfect blend of the two principles
matter and intelligence
If we dismantle an object
breaking them down
into its fundamental particles
we will find intelligence manifest
until the very end
As we delve further, into matter and energy
unearthing gluons, bosons and others
no longer perceptible
subatomic particles, so subtle
reduced to energy pockets
they dissolve into inferences

which, in turn, find their being
in the observer, the I
who, in essence
is self-revealing Consciousness
There is no dividing line
between Consciousness and matter
One does not end for the other to begin
Consciousness never ends, limitless as it is
while matter draws its existence
from the Limitless Being
An apparent togetherness
cause for the manifest and resolved state of creation
Matter, ever changing, is a dependent
with a capacity to reflect
the genius of the Limitless One
Consciousness exists all by Itself
with or without matter
with or without the knower
for both knower and known
derive their existence
from the One Limitless Consciousness
We call the One omniscient
when Its knowledge is viewed
through the entire creation
through all-energy-matter
Consciousness viewed

individually, through the mind
we call it the I, the knower
As for *maya*, the cosmic power
it is ignorance at the individual level
cause of our sense of limitation
making us believe we are bound
to the psycho-physical world
hiding from us the truth
of our limitless nature
In the world around us
we see the process of creation
involving the male and female principles
Extending the process to the cosmic level
moving from the known to the unknown
the twin factors of creation
Consciousness and energy-matter
become the archetypal couple
male and female, father and mother
the Limitless One and Its *maya* power
We look upon the creator
as the universal parent
both father and mother combined
Consciousness we think of as father
the cosmic power as the mother
a divine pair, inseparable
like words and their meanings"

"Energy is a neutral power
Why give it a gender to confuse us?"

"Where the creator is concerned
there is no particular gender
male or female
It includes all the genders
In fact, the wonder of our wise ancestors
they have given us a unique figure
male and female combined
in one human form
ardha-nari in Sanskrit
one half, the masculine force
the other, the gentle femininity
It clearly represents
the divine all-gender encompassing creator
We see in the world around us
it is the female of a species
performing the creator's role
procreating and multiplying
while the role of the male
is hidden and not so obvious
Extrapolating this to the cosmic level
it is *maya's* power at work
everywhere, including our mind and body
It is only natural that we give a gender

to cosmic force of the Limitless One
We as human beings
have a psychological need
for a parental figure
which we can fulfil
in the recognition of a maker
with whom we can resolve
many of our childhood problems
our core issues
referring to our basic unconscious
formed before we turn five
Often we recognise our problems
learn of their workings in our mind
when many years have flown by
our biological parents absent
unavailable or no more
How do we resolve our inner turmoil
locked within our minds?
The One Limitless Consciousness
viewed as both father and mother
as divine parents, god and goddess
personification of love and compassion
the cosmic couple
they are our only help
providing indispensable psychological support
resolving our issues through tears

in their unconditional love
which we longed for from our parents
When our deepest emotions are spent
with our unconscious resolved
we can turn further inwards
towards Truth understanding
with a clear peaceful mind"

Maya and the Individual Mind

"*Maya*, inseparable from the Limitless One
is also the source of our ignorance
The All Pervading Consciousness
must be affected by *maya's* presence
It must eclipse the Limitless One"

"We have explained before
maya's ontological status
It is *mithya*, a dependent-real
It cannot connect with the real
Where is the question of eclipse?
Did the snake or silver exist
to affect the rope or shell?
The Limitless One is all there is
Maya being *mithya*, has no real existence
Maya is the cosmic power
insentient and dependent
on the Limitless Consciousness
It is the source of our ignorance
But, the ignorance is not a real
it is *mithya*, a dependent-real
the result of *maya's* veiling power
How can an apparent existence

hide the intrinsic truth?
It cannot
Its rule stops with our minds
belonging to the same ontological status
The Limitless Intelligence
ignorance cannot touch
Like the sun, that reveals
both itself and the cloud that hides it
the One Consciousness
reveals Itself and ignorance
makes us aware of our knowledge
and of our not-knowing-ness
Maya is the universal energy matter
within time and space
forever changing
How can it hide the One who wields it?
If it really veils Consciousness
there can be neither knowledge nor existence
since we derive our being and intelligence
our capacity to know
from the Limitless One
Just as a mirror shines again
wiped clean of its dust and grime
or a piece of sandalwood
lying in a stagnant pool
its fragrance is not obvious

Once it is cleaned
its perfume is perceptible once again
Fragrance was never really lost
the loss was apparent
as was the gain
of its natural fragrance
The veil of ignorance, a dependent-real
dissolves in the presence of knowledge
revealing the ever present, never absent
self-revealing light
The mind is inanimate matter
limited by time and space
limited by its capacity
Naturally, such a limited mind
if it knows one thing, it cannot know another
at one and the same time
Ignorance is therefore present
from the dawn of creation
We are born ignorant
Our experience proves it
But with every piece of knowledge
the corresponding ignorance vanishes
A peeling away of layers
a step-by-step process
which an alert mind can witness
aware of the disappearance

of a particular not-knowing-ness
But knowledge cannot make the mind omniscient
Just as a searchlight
reveals the objects of its focus
leaves the rest in darkness
a play of light and shade
chiaroscuro of knowledge and ignorance
our mind, subject to *maya's* force
bound by the laws of the world
has both knowledge and ignorance"

"Our minds are products of *maya*
How can insentient products cause knowledge?"

"What we call a mind
is like a mirror that acts as a lamp
by reflecting the light of one
despite having no light of its own
Or like the moon that shines
reflecting the light of the sun
Consciousness illumines the mind
It lights and brings to life
the mind and its activities
Consciousness, like the sun, remains
unaffected by what It illumines
It is the mind that varies

tossed about by its tendencies, its memories
A dust-covered mirror cannot reflect clearly
nor can a convex or a concave mirror
give a true picture of an object
The mind is no different
A disciplined, clear mind
results in better understanding
Just as we use our reflection
despite its dependent-realness
to see ourselves
the mind, despite its dependent-reality
serves to understand and know
the truth of the Limitless One and I"

Individual Understanding

"If as you say everything is the One
There is no other, no two, or more
Non-dual is your opinion
If one person understands the Truth
it stands to reason, the entire universe
must also be released from the I ignorance"

> "No, that is not correct
> I think you have misunderstood
> If what you say is the norm
> if I know German
> the whole world must know it also
> This is not the case; it is not true
> If you need to know German
> you have to learn it, only you
> No one else can do it for you
> The mind with its limited capacity
> is a separate individual entity
> It appears to condition
> the One Consciousness
> Just as a pot, that encloses space
> comes in various sizes and shapes
> the mind appears in infinite varieties

with its own peculiarities
covered by ignorance
needing individual knowledge
to remove the darkness
Just as when one pot breaks
the enclosed space blends, as it were
with all pervading external space
while the other pots remain unaffected
the same is true for the I ignorance
Each person has to learn and understand
the truth of the I, no one else can
There is no such thing
as one person knowing
releasing the universe
from the I ignorance"

Many Minds but One Consciousness

"If minds are separate entities
you have contradicted
your previous theories
Where is the question of One?"

"Yes, minds are many
as are all dependent entities
but Consciousness is one
illumining the world, the creation
including our body and mind
It is the only real
Real as we have shown
there can be just one
An old example to illustrate
many pots but one space
one moon but many reflections
one *satyam* but many *mithya*
You believe that plurality is real
but once you see through and understand
what is the truth, the reality
the plurality, the diversity, disappears
The minds and their infinite varieties
are products of the cosmic *maya*

dependent-reals with apparent existence
As long as you are under *maya's* spell
mesmerised by the marvels of the world
you will take the differences for real
the world, the varieties
the minds, the individual entities
In the wake of knowledge
you will see clearly
the *mithya* status of the world
depending on *satyam*
the one real that is Consciousness
All Pervading Limitless Existence
cause of the universe
This is the essence
of Without a Second"

Helpless Individual

"If everything is the One Consciousness
the entire universe a dependent-real
our body and mind included
a figment of the One's imagination
what happens to us, the individuals?
Helpless puppets of a master puppeteer
where is the need for effort?
Can we drift through life
on the river of fate?"

"No, we cannot drift aimlessly
Life is packed with effort
There is not a moment
when we do not work
Our body functions ceaselessly
if we are to live
Our mind works incessantly
There is no mind without thought
and thinking is an effort
whether we are aware or not
Every second we make a choice
action, no action, a different action
Is this not an effort?

If we choose to drift through life
it is a deliberate choice, an effort
If we choose instead the path of Truth
in search of a solution to our problems
it is also an effort
Unaware of the truth of our 'self'
we separate ourselves from the world
standing apart, isolated, afraid
the world is against us
we are alone, helpless
As my master once said
"The stance of a human
is that of a Ninja"
Ever prepared, a constant alert
unknowing, distrustful of the future
regretting the past
forgetting the present
we spend a life time
elbowing our way through life
a life of constant effort
in search of a permanent solution
a search without understanding
the cause of our problems
that they are born of our not knowing
who and what we are
Since ignorance is the cause

knowledge is the solution
knowledge of our 'self'
When we choose the path of knowledge
Again, it involves effort
We cannot be studio props
in the theatre of the world
We are the actors and act we must
selecting the script of knowledge
Together with our studies
our life style needs to change
our mind, alert and disciplined
contemplative
aware of each and every movement
reaching out to the world
as part of our own being
giving of ourselves completely
not afraid of hurt and healing
knowing the emotions' substance
their fleeting existence
in the light of true understanding"

"How can we discipline our mind?
When each one of our perceptions
is prone to subjectivity?
Every mind is clouded
by traces of prejudice

It is only a matter of degree
An unprejudiced mind does not exist
If Truth understanding
is the only way
it is evident
ego's death is intended
For without a personal point of view
where is the individual?"

"Ego itself is a dependent-real
with no real existence
Where is the question of birth or death?
Realising the truth of the ego
its ontological status
is what we call knowledge
after which there is no I
to state with pride
'I have seen the Truth'
Nor is there a question
"What is to become of me?"
Understanding the ego's reality
results in total objectivity
When we know there is no other
there is no possibility of conflict, no fear
We surrender to the order
accepting what life brings

understanding its fleeting existence
the dependent-realness of the world
yet, alive and alert every moment
This is ego's death
This is total objectivity"

The Importance of a Master

"I agree, understanding the ego's reality
necessitates a study
of our sacred books and scriptures
I can do this on my own
I need not be a parrot
echoing second hand verses
I know the old languages
It should not be difficult
to find out without prejudices
There are many translations
for me to read and know
Where is the need for a master?"

"Unlike other studies
the Truth of the One and I
so easy to misinterpret and misunderstand
you will need a guide
A master who knows without a doubt
with absolute certainty
the meaning of the words
of the *Upanishads* and texts
is the truth of himself
whose knowledge and teaching experience

whose vision and understanding
of the Absolute
of the Limitless One and I
can prevent a world of mistakes
which you will surely make
if the independent path you take
Without a person to teach, as a child
how would you have managed?
Or as an advanced research student
can you cope without a qualified guide?
There is another reason, another aspect
If you need to know the text
you have to proceed gradually
ploughing through each verse or paragraph
To understand each verse or phrase
in depth and in great detail
you need to know
the vision of the entire text
To know the entire text
you have to start from the first
It is a gradual progress
How will you manage without a guide?
Before you ask me, let me pre-empt
A teacher learns from his teacher
right up the line without an end
It is the same as asking

"Who was the first father?"
What will you do for an answer?
A master is a must
learned in the sacred texts
with perfect understanding
a means to communicate
the truth of the world and the One"

"The truth of the world and the One
is only a point of view
It is up to us to choose
from the many points of view"

"No, Truth is not a point of view
There must be a view first
before you have a point or slant
A view by definition
must be the truth, the reality
Truth cannot change
If it does, then, it is not the truth
So, when the words of our sacred texts
repeat endlessly, "You are the whole"
where is the question of interpretation?
When the view itself is the truth
I am the One changeless whole
how can there be points of view?

Besides, if we look at something
from a particular slant
without a complete knowledge of it
we would have to piece together
every point of view and slant
resulting in an imperfect picture
or something unrecognisable
Like the six blind men of Hindustan
who came across an elephant
an animal they had never seen before
Groped their way about
and came to the conclusion
the elephant, from each one's point
was a winnow, a wall, a pillar and so on
Piecing together their perceptions
the elephant would probably resemble
a cubist's abstract representation"

"If I follow the books
I will be just a clone of the master
parroting the master's words"

"If you understand the sacred books
are valid means of knowledge
where is the question of being a clone?
If you believe your eyes or ears

would you say you were mortgaging your mind?
Most definitely not
since they are valid means of knowledge
where the empirical world is concerned
It is the same with the words of the teacher
words from our sacred texts, the *Upanishads*
They are valid means to know
the truth of ourselves
truth we cannot know
without the help of these words
How can we dismiss them
as mere ventriloquism?
If we do, it only shows
we have not clearly understood
the importance of the sacred words
as valid means of knowledge
to know the truth of the knower
the truth of our 'self'"

Are the Sacred Texts Second Hand Knowledge

"I cannot agree with you
No amount of book reading
with or without teachers and teaching
will help us understand the One
Experience is the key to knowing
If we can sit in meditation
watching our breath, in concentration
keeping the mind free of thoughts
in total silence and stillness
this is how we will understand
we are the One Consciousness
Not your books and scriptures
these are just words and more words
better suited to scholars and debaters
Practice is the way, a life of constant alertness
a studied manner we must cultivate
Words and books would be meaningless
without a meditative life
They were and are only second hand knowledge
You need to taste the sugar to know its sweetness
Neither books, nor the wisest of teachers can help

in understanding what is sweetness
The same is true of Consciousness
It can be understood only by experience"

"What you call experience is only knowledge
Touch, taste, smell, sound and sight
together with the mind
bring us knowledge, 'experience', of the world
Every experience must resolve into knowledge
If not we will remain restless
until we know for certain
the content of our experience
When I experience an unknown something
it is recorded in my memory as a feeling
something I sense but do not know exactly
How will I know precisely what that something is?
I have no basis to understand or know
what my experience has shown
Unable to accept an uncertain state
I seek a valid means of knowing
to remove the not-knowing
to help me know with certainty
This is the role of our books and texts
Knowledge is the key
to understand the truth
the Limitless Consciousness and I

the individual conscious being
are one and the same
the source of all creation
If prior to knowledge
through meditation and spiritual exercises
I sense a feeling of oneness
an out of body adventure, a psychic excursion
although, it will leave me bewildered
elated and exhilarated
longing for a repeat performance
I will not be at peace
I will wish to know, with absolute certainty
what I have experienced
I have no choice
Our sacred books and masters
are my only recourse
Through them I can know and understand
the content of my sense of oneness
But if I think that true knowledge
lies in achieving trances and sensations
not in actual knowing or learning
I would be mistaken and there would be
a fatal flaw in my understanding
For every experience is limited by time
Now you have it, and now you do not
Does that not contradict

the meaning of Limitless Existence?
How can I experience the One
when I am already that very same One
although I do not know it?
In every experience the trinity operates
subject, object and the connecting action
the experiencer, experienced and the experience
Who or what lends existence to these?
It can only be the subject
the conscious being, Consciousness
the cause of the world, the universe
To know which we need a valid means of knowledge
bringing us back to our sacred books and texts
Further, what do you mean by 'experience'?
An experience can be any of the three
a contact with an observed fact, an event
or knowledge acquired over time
or an event or occurrence that leaves
an impression in our mind
Normally, we understand experience as an object
as a contact through our mind and senses
When it comes to the Limitless One
we are already that All Pervading Absolute
Where is the question of a contact?
How can the Limitless be an object?
If we mean it is acquired over time

Yes, most certainly, it is a growing clarity
It is not a one-off experience, a flash of discovery
It is a deep understanding born in time
wrought by study and contemplation
When we understand the truth
a complete assimilation, without doubt
it does leave an impression in our mind
Our entire life and outlook changes
with the definite knowledge
People often use the word 'experience'
for this knowledge assimilation
thereby spawning numerous schools
devoted to dividing the ultimate knowledge
into a twin system of theory and experience
cause for confusion and misunderstanding
If we can gain a resolution of the mind
certainly, if it goes along with learning
But, without study, how will we know?
We can, of course, try to gain another high
In the end, we will be none the clearer
Knowledge is, therefore, indispensable
for the sincere seeker of truth
Once it is well understood
there will be no more doubts
no plaguing incertitude"

"The words of our books and texts
reflect others' experiences
We need to find out on our own
by experiencing the truth ourselves
It is not a subject to be taught or learned
for that would make the One an object
Your books are therefore quite redundant"

"An experience, no matter how mystic or elevated
it is momentary, a transient feeling
within time and space, with an ending
If it comes and goes
how can we call it limitless?
Again, as we said before
every experience needs a knower
the experiencer of all experiences
aware of each thought and action
constant witness to our functions
eternal watcher of our mind
To understand the knower, the I
we need a valid means of knowing
Our books and texts now enter
They reveal the I is Consciousness
All Pervading Limitless Consciousness
cause of the entire universe
They continue to explain

how the Limitless Being
manifests as the individual
by a reflection on the mind
the first individuation
separating us from the world
appearing as the I-Am-ness
which in an instant
attaches to the body and mind
identifies with a mental frame
becomes the knower
Duality's genesis
a result of misidentification
taking the dependent for the real
due to beginning-less ignorance
Since ignorance is the cause
for the sense of separation
knowledge must result in union
Although both union and separation
are only apparent
dependent-real in status
an as it were reconnection
due to an as it were disconnection
The I-thought being a reflection
of Consciousness on the mind
it is an apparent combination
of both Consciousness and matter

real and dependent-real
Consciousness is neither subject nor object
It illumines both
But in relation to the I thought
we call It the subject, the I
while the thought itself
is the object
since it involves the mind
It is *mithya*, a dependent-real
How will we come to know on our own
the contrasting elements of the ego?
It is Consciousness expressed through the mind?
Consciousness cannot inform us
It has no action
Nor can it be the individual, the knower
since the I is the subject
to whom knowledge is revealed
Our seeking nature implies
we are ignorant of our 'self'
How will we stop being a seeker?
By ourselves, we can never know
without a doubt
not now, not later
a piquant situation
resolved by our sacred books and texts

the only valid means to know for certain
the truth of the knower, of our 'self'
is the All Pervading Consciousness
cause of the creation"

Can the Self be known

"The 'self' has to be known and understood
as an object of the mind?
The very 'self' that you declared
time and again
it is ever the subject, never an object?
If It is to be known, It is limited
Where is the question of limitlessness?"

"Understanding does not mean
as an object of my mind or senses
It is a mental process
without objectification
As we said before
understanding removes ignorance
It does not create but reveals
the underlying knowledge
When we observe an object
our mind transforms
to correspond to the same object
through form or feeling or both
The knower within, using the memory
identifies the mental frame
"It's a table" or "It's a chair"

This is true of any object or person
situation or emotion
There is the knower, the subject
and the form the mind has assumed
This is the known, the object
In every cognition
there exists the duality
of knower and known, of seer and seen
within time and space
with a form and figure
distinct and concrete
the mind can hold
When it comes to the I, the 'self'
to Consciousness
there are no differences
no distinct object
to recognise
nor is there a need
for a discrete object
since Consciousness is self-evident
requiring no external means
to reveal Its presence
It is a self-revealing light
the basis of our existence
imbuing us with consciousness
making us self-conscious beings

a fact that is self-evident
Understanding the 'self' means
the removal of self-ignorance
revealing the true nature of our 'self'
If we are committed to the pursuit of truth
a disciplined life
a life of study and contemplation
alert and mindful of every thought and action
preparing our mind to absorb the knowledge
then, when the master says
"You are that, dear student"
using subtle logic and words
figures of speech and metaphors
eliding portions of implied sentences
words in apposition and implied negatives
the mind, despite the absence
of something tangible
to transform and correspond
lights up and understands
the meaning of the words
Limitless Existence Consciousness
In that split second
as comprehension dawns
knower-ship and knowing is eliminated
the knower's role negated
the mind is filled and overwhelmed

by the ultimate knowledge
Consciousness alone remains
no duality, no second entity
the 'self' is all there is
This is how we understand the Truth
Not as an object of our mind and senses
not an academic postulate, separate from ourselves
but that the One and I are not different
We are the same Limitless Consciousness
cause of the entire universe"

Is Without a Second a Tautology

"Your point of view, I cannot but think
is mere tautology, a question of semantics
You define the words and go about proving
the very same definitions
in such a roundabout way
It serves more as an intellectual exercise
to keep my intellect alert and agile"

    "Without a Second is no tautology
    The subject is the self-evident I
    to whom the truth is explained
    the truth that the I
    is the Limitless whole
    We need to use words and their nuances
    every argument, every fine difference
    to communicate the vision
    You cannot dismiss them as mere semantics
    Besides, what do you mean by these terms?
    Semantics is a field of study
    relating to words and their meanings
    to help us use the words
    as precisely as possible
    When we wish to convey

the truth of our 'self'
as Limitless Existence
a subject matter so subtle
how can we manage without semantics?
It is a tool, as everything else is
to make us drop the notion
of the limitedness of the I
of the self – evident I
As for tautology
if you mean it is a repetition of facts
by using different words
no, it does not refer to our explanations
But, if we wish to understand with certainty
our sacred books are the only means
to know the truth of our 'self'
These texts reiterate the fact
at every turn, in various contexts
in each of their books
a methodology par excellence
so that we can understand
without a doubt
we are Limitless Consciousness
If you open yourself to the teaching
listen to the words without prejudice
you will understand their power
as you listen in wonder

to the truth of our being
releasing us at once
from the sense of bondage
from limitation and self-non-acceptance
Where is the question of tautology?"

Fate and Suffering

"If the One and I are really one
If as you say, the world is an illusion
as is my mind, my body, all a delusion
I need to make no effort
allowing fate to play her cards
while I remain a pawn
in the game of life
Where is the place in such a scheme
for reaching out to help other beings?
They are only dependent-reals
following fate's order
Should I remain indifferent
to their suffering?
Rationalising, taking refuge
in the laws of cause and effect
in the law of destiny and fate?"

"We have explained at length
the world is neither an illusion nor a delusion
It is ontologically *mithya*, a dependent-real
depending on its cause for existence
We cannot use the knowledge
to abandon our responsibilities

It would be a coward's way out
taking shelter in feeble excuses
The greatest gift we have as humans
is our ability to choose every moment
to act, not act or act in a different manner
A choice we must exercise
within an accepted framework
of universal human values
truth, harmony and non-violence
It will include one's duties
For their performance ensures
the rights of others
A duty-based society is definitely non-violent
conforms best to the order that is the creation
It is up to the individual to act
according to his or her abilities
his or her feelings and sensibilities
They are a part of the order
of the world, the universe
the desire to help
to feel for others' mishaps
Compassion is the hallmark
of all thinking persons
Although, even the most insensitive one
feels a twinge of conscience and emotion
at others' pain and suffering

This is the way of the human heart
the psychological order
reflecting the One's compassion
Its unconditional love and care
Once I know the truth of myself
I am the 'self' of all 'self-s'
I am Limitless Existence Consciousness
There is no 'other' to oppose or limit
How can there be indifference and hatred?
Since the I is all that exists?
It is in fact the most beloved
of each and every individual
For where is the person
who dislikes him or herself?
Every desire, every action
every need to possess
is only because we love ourselves
We love our pleased selves
Although, due to self-ignorance
we think the body and mind is I
Once we know the truth of our 'self'
as the One Limitless Being
How can we remain indifferent?
There is only joy and happiness
love and compassion towards all
There is no further need to acquire

objects, persons and situations
to fulfil ourselves
Free from discontent
from a life of constant 'becoming'
we can give of ourselves completely
without reserve
without a need to gain and withhold
Knowing we are the Limitless whole
we reach out to others
from the fullness of our 'self'"

The Limitless One and God

"Do you mean to say
the laws, the order we see around
the law of cause and effect
is what we term as the almighty?
How can I worship an impersonal energy?"

"When we talk of god, the creator
the cause of the universe
we mean the Limitless One
together with *maya*, Its cosmic power
the totality of everything around
both known and unknown
If we look deeply
probing the world around us
we find an order at work
be it material or ethereal
physical or psychological orders
we as intelligent beings
can discover and understand
Just as from a beautifully crafted sculpture
or an intricately woven cloth
we infer the skill and knowledge
of their talented creator

The world and its magnificence
awe inspiring in its vastness
from the tiny grain of sand
to the immense universe
implies the presence of a maker
with unimaginable intelligence
skill, talent and power
incomprehensible to our limited minds
Such a maker together with the material
the Limitless One and Its *maya* power
we call god, the creator
the almighty father or mother
omniscient, omnipresent protector
The sheer magnitude of the universe
expands our spirit
Songs and words of praise pour out
unasked, from deep within us
Such is the power, the awe
How can we remain unaffected?
How can we not worship it?"

"What is your definition of godhead?
How do we relate to such a one?"

"As we explained earlier
There is just Limitless Consciousness

which, together with Its cosmic power
maya, the universal energy matter
is expressed as the entire creation
The intelligence and the material
we invoke as the godhead
superimposing 'god-ness'
together with forms and names
on the All Pervading Existence
The Limitless One is the real
the One real existent
while *maya*, the source of ignorance
is insentient and dependent
God-ness, like the other 'nesses'
are incidental qualities
superimposed on the Limitless One
Just as water is the truth of the wave and ocean
limitlessness is the truth of the 'self' and the One
Just as the wave relates to the ocean
the ocean to the wave
both in essence being water
with forms and names
we relate to the godhead
the Limitless Consciousness
with an addition of forms and names
A relationship exists
only within the same ontological levels

The godhead and the world
empirically real, relate to one another
while the truth of the world and god
is Limitless Consciousness
As long as we think we are individual beings
the vastness of the creation will dwarf us
We invoke the Limitless One as god
imbuing It with superhuman power
with the best of human qualities
kindness and compassion
We look upon It as father/mother
drawing from It strength and succour"

"The One appears to revel in our sorrows
in our miseries
in a world of violence and disorder
First, it creates this ignorance
Then, it confuses us and draws us
Watches us struggle
as we try to swim homewards
creating whirlpools and eddies
making the effort more difficult"

"We see only disorder and conflict
when we do not know
the truth of our 'self'

when we do not know
who we really are
Once we understand
we are the Limitless Consciousness
we see Its knowledge everywhere
manifest in the order that is the world
If there is a problem
there is a solution
If there is a struggle, there is a reward
It goes hand in hand, the two opposites
If we look at the world with the knowledge
that everything, including our mind and body
is the 'self', the One Consciousness
we find there is such beauty
in the world, an infinite variety
everything in order and in harmony
The diversity sings the glory of the One
When we view the world, the creation
through our wisdom filled eyes
what we used to call as a struggle or sorrow
we call them now as a means to grow
Like our muscles, our physical strength
the more we strain and strive
the stronger we become
through every sorrow and pain
we learn and we grow

in our minds, in our emotions
more at peace
with those around
Although at the moment of suffering
life does seem hard
This is when prayers help
We turn to god
helping us to recall
the Without a Second knowledge
all that there is, is the Limitless One
speaking through Its compassion
Its infinite grace
giving us space
a proper perspective
to life's many problems"

Compassionate God in Heaven

"In your scheme of things
the One merely watches
the world and the inequalities
whereas god in heaven, the almighty father
he feels for me
One day, when the world I leave
I shall be a part of him and his glories
How can I replace this joy
with the One's indifference?"

"As we said earlier
the Limitless One with Its *maya* power
the All Pervading One with forms and names
is what we call god, the almighty creator
The world order reflects
the order that we call god
the order that is the creation
choreographed so perfectly
this enormous universal production
His presence, his knowledge
is everywhere visible
in the laws and orders of the universe
making them work, making them intelligible

This is what we call god's grace and blessing
Imagine our lives if the laws of physics turn volatile
fire turns cold and the water flies
if the order of ends and means do not coincide
nor do the laws of cause and effect
We wake up each morning
with anxiety and trepidation
not knowing what is the day's surprise
We would be absolute nervous wrecks
If this is not grace
I ask you, what is?
Next, if god is away
he being the omnipotent, omnipresent
omniscient eternal one
We can never ever be one with him
He is located in a specific place
far away from our troubles
Where he is, we are not
where we are he cannot be
It certainly contradicts
the meaning of omnipresent
as it does the word 'eternal'
It is the here and now
without time or change
ever present, that is what we call

Limitless Eternal Existence
There cannot be a separation or union
We have to be the Limitless One, here and now
There is neither a becoming nor a joining
either now or later, for it would mean
a disjoining in the future
gaining and losing imply a time factor
time does not, cannot have a role
where eternity is concerned
The Limitless One is beyond time, as we said earlier
It is the very basis of both time and space
How are we going to be any better
knowing that our being a part of god
will be for a short time, no matter what?
Just as we spend what we have earned
depleting our bank balances in turn
it cannot be any different in heaven
The only difference could be
we will spend not money but merit
gathered from the good deeds on earth
Once the merit that took us to heaven
is exhausted and spent
back to the earth or further down we will go
The law of destiny will once again flow
Another flaw I must point out

the formless god has a location?
How is this possible?
It is against any logic or reason
If he is omnipresent, he cannot have a form
Formless as he is how can you confine him?
You have not thought through your definitions
Otherwise, you would not have located him
so far away, safe and secure from your coils
If you need attributes
everything you see here, every colour
every shape, form and figure
every single attribute and more
is god, the omnipresent creator
If we can return to our previous explanations
the Limitless One together with Its *maya* power
manifests as the many, as the world
without a change or action
neither an increase nor a decrease
It remains as it is, the same as I, the 'self'
indivisible, complete and full
Limitless, Existence, Consciousness
When the entire universe
is the One Consciousness
which when seen from creation's point
we call god, the cause, the creator

tell me, where is not god?
In the creation, what is not god?
What greater joy can there be
knowing there is only god?"

The One without Attributes

"Our minds cannot comprehend
things that have no qualities or attributes.
I agree It is One, but with a difference
It is One with infinite divine attributes"

    "If the Limitless One has attributes and qualities
    how does It relate to them?
    Does It own or possess these qualities
    as a man does a house or property?
    If that is true
    what is the real nature of the Limitless One?
    If the One is the qualities and attributes
    these qualities change constantly
    our experiences prove it definitely
    the Limitless One Itself must change
    since It is the attributes
    How can we call such a changeable principle, Limitless?
    Where is the question of omnipresence
    omniscience and all pervasiveness?
    The words would be meaningless
    If the One is to be the ever-present
    Limitless principle
    it cannot have attributes or qualities

for they will limit the Limitless Being
The Limitless One, like the sunlight
untouched by what It reveals
blesses the entire creation
the infinite varieties
while It remains a witness
to Its myriad powers
Such a One is what we call
Limitless Existence Consciousness
Another problem of your hypothesis
if the One has only divine attributes
who has the non-divine ones?
How will you explain the problems
we see in the world?
To whom do they belong?
To the Limitless One? To us?
Your definition of the One has no answer
We have to turn to Without a Second
to the Limitless One without attributes
which lends existence
but remains untouched
If we look around us, the entire creation
we can see the One's All Pervading presence
It appears as the many, without changing
such as clay, gold, space in a vessel
other examples we have used

For, what we call god
is the Limitless One with Its *maya* power
pervading the entire creation
Every aspect is blessed as god's manifestation
As for understanding the Limitless One
the attribute-less Being
we cannot understand It
as an object of our mind
We know we are self–conscious beings
It is a self-evident fact
We need no external revelation
to reveal
our self-evident self-consciousness
But, to understand the equation
between our 'self' and the Limitless One
we need the words of our sacred books
When the master, learned in the scriptures
using every pedagogic tool he has
takes us through the learning
step by step until we understand
there is just one
without parts or attributes
It is the one real existent
all the rest are *mithya*, dependent-reals
the One All-Pervading
Limitless Existence Consciousness

the basis of the entire universe
is the same as the I, the 'self'
we will understand without a doubt
This is the final comprehension
setting us free from the I ignorance
free from the sense of limitation
total freedom in every way"

Is Creation a part of God

"Your explanations do not address
the question of happiness
the eternal bliss we arduously seek
How can the formless One help us?
We are a part of the All Pervading One
It is through prayers and devotion
we dissolve into the Divine
inseparable, bathed in eternal bliss"

    "How can eternal bliss begin?
    A beginning implies an end
    It involves time
    Eternity is not within time
    If we are to be eternally happy
    we must be so, here and now
    not sometime in the future
    'Now' is the only eternal bliss
    By happiness, we mean
    a sense of complete being
    whole, without a division
    But according to you
    you are a part of the Limitless One
    It is true, we are parts

we are a part of the creation
a creation that is *mithya*, dependent-real
It includes our body and mind
We are part of the *mithya* creation
How can we be a part of the Limitless One?
How can *mithya* be a part of *satyam*?
If all that you seek
results in your being
a part of the All Pervading One
you will remain a distinct separate person
retaining your identity, your individual 'self'
No matter how subtle the difference
a difference, it still is
Even the slightest separation causes a split
Your mind divided, a conflict ensues
A mind in conflict brings in its wake
restlessness, anxiety and mental pain
A division between the One and you
between you and the rest
where is your happiness?
If misery and discontent were our nature
we would welcome them with open arms
neither seeking relief nor questioning our lot
But the fact is we are permanent seekers
in our persistent quest for happiness
which proves our misery, our helplessness

is not our natural state
Whereas when we are happy
we are whole, we are content
with no desire to disturb the moment
Which person would wish to trade
his happy state to one of discontent?
We seek this elusive bliss
all through our life
It seems to be the only reason
to keep ourselves alive
seeking it in blessed sleep
or in that moment of joy
when our hopes are fulfilled
where no division, no split exists
Where is the question of parts?
When the mind is at peace, it is whole
This is what we call happiness or bliss
A whole, undivided mind can exist
only with the awakening
of Without a Second knowledge
I am the All Pervading Spirit
without want, without limit
with no 'other' to restrict
my limitlessness
the essence of my 'self' "

Is God affected by the Creation

"You bring god down to our level
by using cause and effect
many tools of logic
God's will cannot be questioned
He is beyond our limited power of reason
Whereas according to your contention
god and we are identical
If your interpretation is the truth
why do we have such conflicts?
Why such misery, such violence?
The One must be affected
by all the problems, ours and the rest's"

"The One is not affected by Its creation
Like the sunlight, revealing everything
It remains untouched and bright
serene and unwavering
Violence and conflict
animate and inanimate
are all revealed by the Limitless One
No pollution or environmental degradation
can desecrate space
It is the same with Consciousness

Untouched by what It reveals
It supports the entire universe
We have explained at length
the ontological status of the world
It is *mithya*, dependent-real
Where is the question of connection
between the Limitless One and the creation?
Satyam can never be affected by *mithya*
How can the Limitless One be affected
by the world, its creation?
What you term as god's will
is the order that is the creation
the order of cause and effect
the order of ends and means
There is no asking why and where
It is the cause and effect order
It is just and fair
We see around us, the order at work
in every aspect of our life
It is the same as asking
why the sun should rise
every day from the east side?
Why not for a change
rise from the west?
It would be as ludicrous

If god's will is beyond comprehension
how will you explain the chaos
the confusion reigning around us?
It would make god whimsical
blessing some and damning others
How can we rely on a whimsical being?
It most certainly cannot be godhead
If we look through the apparent chaos
we find there is order in the world
Every effect has a cause
every end a means
whether we know it or not
The misery, pain and violence
are effects of various causes
mingling of fate and free-will
destiny and psychology blended
Given the law and order
of the created world
we are responsible
for the rights and wrongs
using or abusing our gift of free-will
In other life forms
it is more an instinct
the will to survive
nature's programming

to propagate the species
In a human being
a gift of deliberate choice
weighing the options
choosing one
discarding the others
a choice of ends and means
this precious gift
specially endowed to us
is meant for use with care"

"How do we know
if it is fate or free-will that decides?"

"It is an age-old debate
the question of free-will or fate
There is an order of cause and effect
We see it working everywhere
although we don't deliberate
or take notice of it
If we do, we must accept
a past action gives a present result
Extending the order to life beyond
what we call as fate today
is the result of our free-will
exercised yesterday

A past life's action fructifies in the present
Logic, we can definitely accept
since it follows the laws of cause and effect
Although we may not know the reason
the fact remains there is one
An effect must have a cause
The universal law of cause and effect
does not depend on our whims
to prove its existence
That it exists we cannot but accept
A person's past actions, in a previous life
his hopes, his unfulfilled desires
his hurt and pain given or gained
of which he has no remembrance
decide his birth, his genetic code
the many different situations
destiny for him unfolds
If we live questioning every moment
if it is fate or free-will that takes precedence
we would be wasting away precious moments
The two forces together decide the results
We enter this world with a certain predisposition
talents, bent of mind and predilection
flavours from our past lives
To achieve our potential we have to act

We have to choose to do or not
Fate cannot play its cards
without us, the player
Fate itself follows an order
ordained by the creator
Destiny has dealt us the cards
time, place, family and circumstance
It is our game; we have to make the moves
with a definite win or loss at the conclusion
This is where fate plays its part
We have a choice laid out for us
a life of acquisition and success
or a life of study and contemplation
discipline and renunciation
If the end we wish to pursue
is knowledge of the truth
we must choose a life style
appropriate to our desire
since ends and means must align
to achieve the chosen goal
There will be obstacles
numerous hidden variables
over which we have no control
since we cannot even know
who or what they are
But patience and devotion

a single-minded approach
can surmount even the steepest slope
Of our own free-will and effort
we must work towards our chosen goal
without anxiety of the future result
to divert our attention
Mindful of the process, of the details
offering our effort as a mark of devotion
understanding the results
are a blend of free-will and fate
we accept them with grace
as blessings of the One Limitless
We maintain an emotional balance
through our life of mixed results
winning some and losing others"

"How do we know what is right or wrong
without being taught?
Life is rarely black or white
Situations we face are often so fluid
life is invariably in shades of grey
Can we ever escape the clutches of fate?"

"Right or wrong we can sense, instinctively
a reason we call it universal
If education is required

it stands to reason
it will not be available for everyone
Including some and excluding others
it would imply a defect in the order
the order that is the creation
a charge both invalid and baseless
Universal values, the ones we commonly sense
not-hurting-ness and truth
applies to all people in all situations
These of course have to be fine-tuned
to suit individual roles and situations
Modified values, specialised values
differ according to each person
his or her age, status, occupation
time, place, culture and so on
For these modified rights and wrongs
we need help, advice and counsel
But the universal rights and wrongs
every human being knows
Yet, due to emotional pressures
we choose to ignore them
consciously, but more often mechanically
thereby gathering many 'fruits of actions'
turning ourselves over
into the ready hands of fate
the law of cause and effect"

The Problem of Nothing-ness

"Why do you define reality as One?
Since one devoid of attributes
is really a nothing-ness
why not a zero or a cipher?
Better still, a void, emptiness?"

"If the All Pervading Being
is a void, a nothing
how will you explain the fact of existence
of yourself and the world?
If you and the world do not exist
there cannot be a void
since there is no one to declare
'The Truth is emptiness'
If we use the logic of cause and effect
an effect must reflect its cause
A mango tree cannot sprout
from the seed of a tamarind
Then, how can the world
be created from nothing?
It will negate all existence
If as you say it is a void
which means each one of us

is emptiness
how will we ever know
we are 'nothing'?
Since we do not exist?
We enter this path of knowledge
in search of ending our grief
which leads us to inquire
into the reality of our being
of who and what we are
As we look into ourselves
we find we are complete, content
with no further want or need
no desire to change or transform
when we are happy
when we have achieved what we desired
Further delving into this state of mind
we find there is no division, no split
between the wanting me and the desired object
Both the subject and object are one
It is the same oneness
when we hear an amusing anecdote
We laugh unreservedly
letting ourselves go
There is no thought of the self-judging ego
For the moment, it is forgotten

Joy that is our intrinsic nature
bursts forth as uninhibited laughter
The feeling of joy, of 'fullness'
so wonderful and pleasing
we long to extend the emotion
The start of an endless search
a life of constant 'becoming'
seeking an 'eternal bliss'
a never-ending feeling of happiness
Finally, care worn and exhausted
from our hopeless quest
we are forced to seek solace and rest
Now begins a new search
for spiritual paths and teachers
When the same teachers tell us
"You are emptiness
there is no existent 'self'
Emptiness is the truth
As is the path so is the goal
the means, the very end
Practice is the key
to the perfection you seek
You have nothing to hold on to
except the regimen of practice"
Can you truly accept without chagrin

such an advice or counsel?
It would negate your entire search
because prior to your seeking
you have already experienced
a sense of being complete and whole
But the teaching now negates
your very experience
the basis of your turning a seeker
You cannot accept the words
It goes against all reasoning
since you will definitely question
the reasons for the teaching
You will ask, naturally
how did creation emanate from nothing?
What is the basis for such a conclusion?
If nothing-ness is the truth, the reality
the world you have to negate
as an illusion, a false appearance
These are relative terms
requiring an absolute
to give the words a meaning
Without an absolute
where is the question of illusion?
or false existence?
If reality, the Absolute, is a void

the *mithya* creation becomes a real
You are then bound to this world
since reality cannot change
Where is the question of liberation?
With further contemplation
you will have to ask this next question
Who is aware of the nothing?
Who or what makes the emptiness known?
What is its basis?
For every postulate and idea
derives its existence from a conscious source
Consciousness in essence
In despair, you will have to turn
to Without a Second
where the sacred books and texts
speak without a doubt
the truth is one, non-dual
Limitless Existence Consciousness
This and this alone will end your search"

"In creation, everything is empty of its 'self'
be it an object, an emotion or a person
Without innate existence, they are empty
For instance, what is a chair?
Is it the seat, the backrest or the legs?
Is it the wood from which it is made?

If we remove the parts, there is no chair
If we remove the wood
obviously, there can be no chair
A chair, then, has no real existence
There is nothing called a chair
just name, form and function
put together for the moment
It has no intrinsic being
This is what we mean by emptiness
Emptiness has neither dualities nor cause and effect
neither opposites nor subject object divisions
Emptiness is the essence of the creation, of our being"

"Does the emptiness exist
or is it empty of existence?
Since you say that everything is emptiness,
'emptiness is'
Emptiness obviously has an existence
Being existent, what does it rest on?
What supports the emptiness?
As we have explained before
we know that existence implies
an already existing conscious being
There can be no other answer
Emptiness must rest on Consciousness
Limitless Existence Consciousness

If your reply is that emptiness
is an absence of dualities of forms and names
of relative terms and opposites
it is without subject or object
without pairs of opposites
although you do not use the exact word
what else can it be but the Absolute?
Once you have the Absolute
which, as we have explained before
Is Limitless Existence Consciousness
every aspect of the creation
is understood as *mithya*, dependent-real
depending on Limitless Consciousness
to give it an existence
When you say the world is emptiness
it cannot be different from *mithya*
But, when you extend the term
to include the truth
without positing an absolute
emptiness has no meaning
If, however, you persist in your thesis
the world is an illusion, empty of existence
the truth of creation is 'emptiness'
we must ask you
what is the nature of emptiness?

Who is aware of the emptiness?
What will be your response?"

"How is your dependent-reality different
from declaring the world an illusion?
You negate earthly existence
with stating there is only one real
Limitless Consciousness"

"The term dependent-real or *mithya*
has been explained before
It does not negate
the existence of the world
It is an empirical reality, subject to change
existing within time and space
within its given time
It has a form, name and a purpose
We can use it for transaction
to serve our various ends
Body, mind, objects, people
in short, the entire creation
comes under this category
of dependent-reals
depending on the Limitless Consciousness
There is no question of negation or illusion
We understand the reality of the world

of our body and mind
as *mithya*, dependent-real
in relation to the Absolute
in relation to Its essential nature
Limitless Existence Consciousness"

Mystic Experience and Knowledge

"If the One and you are the same
the One with form or without
where is the question of grace?
Who is to bless; who is to receive?
You have no soul, no divine Muse
Your logic has dried her very spirit
You can never imagine, much less conceive
the lofty heights a mystic experience can bring
leaving us longing for more and more
of god's love, his divine bliss
Despite your protests, I still think
Without a Second makes you proud
to the point of arrogance"

"There is no pride in declaring
a fact, the truth
If I emphatically state
two and two make four
If I stand by my statement
refusing to alter my stand
does it make me arrogant?
Besides, arrogance and humility, both
arise from an alienated ego

alienated from the Limitless One
I have tried to explain
the differences between
real and dependent-real
satyam and *mithya*
There can be just One real
that is Limitless Consciousness
Naturally, the manifest world
is understood as apparent, as *mithya*
the individualities as dependent-reals
The I, identical with the One, in essence
is realised as the cause of the world
By stating a fact, incredible as it may sound
to those who do not know
how can it make me arrogant?
As for your mystic experiences
it is wonderful reading
their content, however is incomplete
No matter how poetic they be
how can they help in knowing?
Truth has a beauty all its own
Only in its absence, we have shrouded words
with an aroma of wisdom
to capture souls
yearning for experiences
beyond the common and the ordinary
Besides, finding the right teacher

understanding the teaching
both require grace
which we have to earn
through prayers and actions
Grace gives us the desire and the means
to know the truth of ourselves
that we are at once
both the 'blesser' and the blessed
Our present good fortune
results from grace earned in the past
Knowledge may seem matter of fact
without the heady flavour of romance
very mundane and down to earth
yet, they convey and teach
with clarity and lucidity
helping you see clearly
the truth of one's being
It brings with it love and compassion
caring and consideration
a total connection with the rest of the world
We are inter-beings we cannot deny
inter-related in every way
Knowing that all that we see around
including my body and mind
are not different
from the One Limitless Consciousness

how can we have dislikes and prejudices?
A separation, distinction of yours and mine?
Seeking freedom from bondage
must give way to seeking knowledge
For total freedom means
knowledge of the truth
Knowledge may seem to lack a soul
according to our romantics
but I would not change it
for a world of poetic verses
However, if you mean by experience
a total assimilation of the truth
I have no contention
with your choice of words
except that the word 'experience'
can convey something quite different
It could make your listeners
pursue various techniques
in search of the 'eternal bliss'
without understanding
the meaning of 'eternal'
It could negate your entire teaching
We can never over emphasise
the importance of knowledge
in understanding the Truth of the I
as Limitless Consciousness"

The Role of Forms and Rrituals

"If we are god
if we are the Limitless One
why do we have forms and prayers?
Even your most ardent supporter
composes words of praises
extolling the virtues of a godhead
Does it not contradict your thesis
you are the Limitless All Pervading Being?"

"No, there is no contradiction
It calls for better understanding
In every race and culture
forms and prayers are guides
a focus, a light
to steer young minds
foster the right values
the right attitudes
devotion and discipline
Prayer and prayerfulness, both
born of complete free-will
freest of our actions
they can never be forced
We can assume false airs

present a picture of prayerfulness
How can we disguise our mind?
We pray only because we wish to
voluntarily, from our heart
The sacred hymns and rituals
join together, in chorus
our physical, mental and vocal actions
Prayers and forms of worship
remind us at every stage
our body and mind's mortality
its limitedness
and the inter-connectedness
of the empirical world
the time and space enveloped world
The laws of cause and effect, ends and means
penetrate every aspect, every corner
from the micro-sub-atomic level
to the macrocosm of the universe
All actions gross and subtle
affect this dynamic network
like the flapping of a butterfly's wings
can create a storm in New York
Every action produces an effect
equal to, more than or less than our wishes
The result could also be just the opposite
But, results and effects they definitely produce

Prayers and rituals are no different
They are actions, deliberate actions
They definitely yield results
as they ripple across the web
of laws and orders of the world
The immensity of the universe
of the Limitless One and Its *maya* power
makes us understand, with greater force
the magnitude of the knowledge
the essential oneness of our 'self'
and the All Pervading Consciousness
A humbling experience
we turn with reverence
reaching out to the infinite grace
of the All Pervading One
invoking It with prayer and devotion"

"By invoking the One in a form
are we not limiting the Limitless One?"

"No, we are not limiting the limitless
Our minds cannot comprehend
the vastness of the creation
We need a form to focus
a form to guide us
but, it is not the form we worship

We are not idol devotees
It is the Limitless we invoke
as god or goddess
in forms and symbols
with sacred chants and rituals
Imbued with our faith and devotion
the form becomes a source of power
from which we draw succour
a mutual two-way transaction
sustaining the devotee and his devotion
If we understand clearly
forms are symbols
not the absolute real
they will help us expand our minds
But, if we take the form as the real
revering our choice, rejecting others'
declaring with belligerence
one form's supremacy over the rest
a reflection of our mind's limitedness
resulting in fanaticism and narrow mindedness
we commit the gravest of errors
we limit the Limitless"

The Ideal Seeker of Truth

"From our discussions it is evident
the one who enters Without a Second
must be pragmatic, objective
of clear mind, intelligence and reason
with a single-pointed desire for truth
who has a rich sense of discrimination
values, ethics and moral obligation
This means it precludes
the majority of human kind
What is the use of such knowledge?
When it blesses a few and condemns the rest?
I would far rather choose
the path of prayer and devotion
It is open to every person
no matter what the level of intelligence"

"You are partially right, there
Without a Second does need maturity
a degree of independence and objectivity
Although these are not our present qualities
they can be cultivated as we go along
It is therefore open to all seekers of truth
What is required, is a thirst for knowledge

an unquenched desire to know the real
a life of discipline, a sense of duty
together with devotion, some humility
discrimination, a questioning mind
clearly thinking through to a logical end
caring and compassion
courage and determination
measured speech and integrity
These are the traits of a mature person
who with the passage of time
can absorb and understand
the precious knowledge that is Without a Second"

"How do we get this knowledge
clear and thorough, without doubts?
By what means and techniques?"

"An excellent understanding
of right and wrong
unswerving from the path of truth
a relentless pursuit of *dharma*
of the order, of what is right
an absolute must
managing our likes and dislikes
consequently our hurt and guilt
the two greatest enemies

of mental peace
We need a constant vigil
watching our mental patterns
to understand the working of our mind
In each of our actions
a small step astray, a slight distraction
our alertness must come to play
bringing the errant mind back to stay
observing our thoughts without prejudice
without judgement or condemnation
neither guilt nor hurt nor regret
letting go gently
each and every thought
with love and compassion for all
including ourselves
knowing that every emotion
every aspect of the creation
every thought and action
is I, every hurt and guilt
yet, I am none of these
understanding very well
everything is the order
the order of the creation
including our psyche
By observing our mental patterns
gradually, over years, we come to understand

the inner world within ourselves
resulting in a disciplined life
simplicity which is concomitant
with a thirst for the Ultimate
To remind ourselves at every step
the truth of the Limitless One and I
prayers, meditation and other practices
are aids to help us bring the teaching into our life
It is in the practices, we find many varieties
misleading some to believe
there are many philosophies
It is neither true nor correct
There are innumerable variations
in each and every individual
different capacities, talents
preferences and bent of mind
circumstances and opportunities
of various kinds
Each one can choose a path
of practice and discipline
according to his or her preference
a practice all their own
reacting and responding individually
to life's various situations
We can therefore say
there are as many methods and ways

of discipline and practice
as there are people
but not many truths or realities
nor many points of view
People often mistake
the practice for the knowledge
an obvious misconception
for how can we practice reality?
How can we experiment
with Limitless Conscious Being?
Do we need practice
to know we are human beings?
Should we constantly chant and repeat
'I am human, I am human'
for us to understand this fact?
Where Truth is concerned
Reality, a question of the Absolute
it is not a theory; it cannot be practised
it is a fact to be known and understood
A path and practice are required
for preparing the mind
to lead a contemplative life
removing the mind's many habits
acquired and carefully nurtured
over thousands of life-times
It is, naturally, a gradual process

    practice and patience
    study and deep devotion
    to bring about Truth assimilation"

"Then, time is a factor
where knowledge is concerned
It is only after we practice
can we truly understand
the truth of the One and I"

    "Time is a factor, yes
    for disciplines and practices
    not for knowledge and understanding
    The moment you understand
    you will know the truth, instantly
    There is no question
    of completing one action
    before another begins
    Knowing and understanding
    are not sequential; they are instantaneous
    If we split a log into two
    is there a time gap
    between the actual splitting
    and obtaining two pieces of wood?
    There is no lapse of time
    It is instantaneous

Knowledge is no different
The moment you know
your understanding is complete
Although knowledge is instantaneous
we require study and discipline
preparing our mind
to receive and assimilate this knowledge
Our mind, like a Polaroid picture
grows in clarity
with maturity and wisdom
until it is ready to understand and absorb
the truth of the I and the Limitless One"

"Why is it, there are so few
who seek this knowledge?
What is it that draws them?"

"Blessings earned from a past life
make some people contemplative
observant and objective
They stop to ask and inquire
the how and why of their minds
It gives them a sense of balance
a capacity to shoulder responsibilities
with maturity and care
analysing human nature

their activities and aspirations
Questioning through, they seek out
the reasons, the causes and effects
of individual behaviour
the constant desire to change
our status and our attire
the constant urge to acquire
people, emotions, objects and power
imagining that the fulfilment of our desire
will bring us the happiness
we assiduously seek
Their analysis tells them the motif
instigating all human actions
the basic desire for freedom
be it from sorrow or dissatisfaction
from a sense of incompleteness
from frustration or even despair
Yet, despite the effort
freedom remains elusive
or at best, a palliative
a solace for the moment
to start all over again
a cycle without beginning or end
A mature person sees the futility
the wasted effort of most human activity
thinks through and wonders

if there is no end to a life of seeking
He or she, then, seeks an answer
Their life they dedicate
to find a solution to our 'becoming' life
a permanent solution that ends our search
With resolve, they spend their life
questioning, analysing, with a clear mind
a life of study and contemplation
Masters, sacred books and scriptures
prayers, rituals and meditation
help them sustain
their desire for sufferings' end
to persevere until they understand
the truth of the 'self'
discovering with wonder
that freedom is our very nature
for we are not different
from the Limitless One
It is obvious, then, there can be
just a few who so dedicate their lives
We cannot know for certain
the exact reason
why some enter and not others
the path of knowledge and truth
It is more a probability
their individual destiny

unfolding in time
   a question of goodness
   divine grace or blessing"

"Once they have understood the truth
how do such persons transact with the world?
What are their values, their attitudes?
What is the one that sets them apart?"

   "Their lives of course are exemplary
   bringing hope to an otherwise hopeless world
   We can learn from their attitudes
   truth, non-hurting, caring and gentleness
   compassion and towards all, a friendliness
   maturity and a total objectivity
   discrimination and balance
   gentle at all times, but when needed
   very firm and decisive
   free from the stranglehold
   of preferences and prejudices
   cheerful, spreading warmth
   dynamic, people flock to them
   drawn by their magnetic presence
   enthusiastic, ever ready to help those in need
   yet, alert to pretence and hypocrisy
   living in this world, using its wealth as a trustee

>   ready to let go without possessing
>   an expansive heart, embracing all beings with love
>   and many more we cannot enumerate every one
>   Of all these, the one that leads the rest
>   ahimsa, non-hurting-ness
>   avoiding all hurting actions
>   physical, mental or verbal
>   is the one that stands out the best
>   It is the guiding principle
>   the foundation of their life"

"Ahimsa, non-hurting-ness, a common word
What does the value signify
that you choose it over the rest?"

>   "Every other value and attitude
>   can be reduced to non-hurting-ness
>   Every action that disturbs
>   the rhythm, the harmony of the world
>   is violence, no matter how subtle
>   When we mislead another, it is a hurt
>   trivial or serious, we cannot judge
>   Pride, anger, envy, theft
>   greed, conceit, mal-intent
>   hatred, enmity, possessiveness
>   acquisitiveness, hoarding miserliness

hypocrisy, subterfuge and others
including topical values
neglecting or desecrating the environment
inappropriate behaviour and appearance
lack of punctuality, politeness and tact
every action against the order around us
causes violence, conflict and hurt
however subtle or imperceptible
to our untrained eyes
It is not easy to decide
the time, place, the how-s and when-s
of appropriateness and right actions
but, with alertness and practice
keen observation and sensitivity
with balance and harmony as watchwords
we can avoid many an unconscious hurt
without compromising integrity and truth
The one value that stands out
in the life of a person who has understood
ahimsa, non-hurting-ness
is the all pervasive value
including every other there is
It is the touchstone of maturity"

What does Death mean for the Wise

"No matter however wise
as long as we have a body and mind
we can never be totally free
If this is true, what happens to the wise?
Do they die the moment they understand
they are not different from the One?"

"Birth and death belong to the relative world
A wise person looks upon death
as the dropping away
of one's psycho-physical self
for what is born, one day must die
It is the order of creation
When the physical body 'dies'
it returns to the five elements
bones to the earth, fluids to the water
warmth to the fire, breath to the wind
the space within the body, the space it occupied
to the elemental space
As for the mind, the thoughts and memories
together with the identity-giving ego
for the person who knows the truth
the 'self' is the Limitless One

like water sprinkled on a burning hot stone
they evaporate leaving behind no trace
Without the ego, there is no identity
No one to own up the thoughts and memory
arresting forever all future births
For one who knows the truth
he or she knows there is just One real
the rest are dependent-reals
including the body and mind
existing within time and space
Bodies and minds change
it is their nature, being dependent-reals
but I, the One, the only real
Limitless Existence Consciousness
was, is and will be always
just existence, with neither birth nor death
For what is limitless, how can it die?
If every sage and wise person
should cast off their body
the moment he or she understands the truth
where will we find masters to teach?
How will we find a way out of our sorrow?
But we do have masters to teach
to lead and guide us to our 'self'
The answer to your question is obvious
Death is *not* the hallmark of the wise"

"When a wise person's body falls away
what happens to the fruits of his or her actions?
Do they not have to experience them?
After all, as long as their body exists
they think and act like the others"

"Once a person understands the truth
his or her past 'fruits of actions'
accumulated in their many births
are completely wiped out
not a trace of them remains
Only that 'fruit of action'
because of which they have a body
continues to function
until the body falls apart
But the results of their actions
performed in this life
no longer adheres to them
They have no sense of doer-ship
having understood clearly
the *mithya*, dependent-real status of their ego
Their lives are instruments of the Lord
empty flutes, playing his divine song
in complete harmony with the world"

For Those who do not Know

"What happens to those
who die without knowing the truth?"

"People who do not know
are not even aware of the truth
the triple knot of ignorance
binds them to the world
At first, the ignorance veils their thinking
making them identify with their body and mind
separating them from the rest of the world
Unable to accept the isolation
since it is not the truth of the 'self'
they yearn to fulfil themselves
to feel complete and whole
The yearning turns to desire
urging them to act
often without prudence
tossed by their preferences
They choose their fancies
over their duties
unable to loosen the hold
of their conflicting emotions

resulting in their gaining some merit
but more often than not
many liabilities and failings
These are the 'fruits of their actions'
which, after death, propel them to seek
a different form, a different scheme
to fulfil their unfulfilled hopes and dreams
or experience the result of their past deeds
a never-ending cycle of birth and death
ceaselessly pursuing transient goals
until frustrated, full of despair
they turn to seek solace
in one of their many births
a chance earned
through some past good deed
the start of their spiritual journey
a tentative beginning
to end the cycle
of birth and death"

The Wonder that is Without a Second

"Without a Second, by your definition
gives the world an apparent existence
You see it, you touch it; you can feel it
yet you can live untouched by it
because, in essence
it has no real existence
It seems to me that it lacks spirit
to live a life, tasteless and insipid
It takes the joy out of living"

"On the contrary, Without a Second
makes life so extraordinary, so fresh
knowing there is just One Existent
One Eternal Consciousness
performing different roles
as the ego, knower, body and mind
names, forms, animate, inanimate
an infinite variety, a divine entertainment
appearing as the many, as it were
illumining my mind
breathing it with life
making it aware of the world

It is the life of our life, the eye of our eye
What greater wonder can you expect?
seeing things just as they are
with neither flights of fancy
nor spiritual romanticism
with a capacity to look and admire
Its works, Its immense power
Free from psychological shackles
there is no more self-non-acceptance
An emotional dwarf, I shrank from people
cocooned in a shroud of low self-esteem
These made me a seeker of varied experiences
I hoped for respite, a certain peace of mind
drowning my cares in haze filled moments
Little did I know such joy existed
as the knowledge that I am the Limitless One
I am the Limitless Consciousness
the All-Pervading Existence
the cause of the universe
I feel as though a burden
has vanished from my heart
In spite of my body and mind
in spite of the pains of the world
my spirit soars like a bird in flight
I look around with wonder filled eyes
carefree, joyful, innocent as a child

a feeling of love, of compassion
for every living creature, every single being
enveloping them in a loving embrace
their highs and lows, their joys and pains
aware they are not different from me
yet I am untouched; I am free
alert impartial observer of the world
I did not know nor hoped to see
the wonders that lie before me
Every moment an eternity
I live, dwell in it wholeheartedly
with no thought of past or future
the now is all that matters
seeing the world as it is
accepting the realities
without judgement or prejudice
No longer does my memory impede
projecting, superimposing from its files
creating a rift between me and the world
I see clearly the miracle of reality
of life and its many splendours
with liquid crystal eyes
When your life reflects the truth
when every breath and being
echo the words' meaning
"You are that, dear student"

the same wonder will be yours
We can share in the joy of the world
in its waves, swim and swirl
until, like bubbles to the ocean
we merge into the Limitless One
Although in truth, there is no merging
nor emerging, for we are the same
It is a matter of definite knowing
There is no coming or going
It is a question of being
of course understanding
I am One with the One
in each and every way
Never apart, I never really was
It was all an appearance
Now I have woken from this dream
Oh, what a wonder! I can truly see
There is no world, nobody
nothing other than me
I know now that everything
is the One's *maya* appearing
The mind relaxes in the knowing
The ego's games I watch, laughing
aware that it has lost its hold
on me for ever more
I find the world smiling

as firm is the understanding
there is no other
All is just the One
Dearly Beloved
Eternal Spirit . . . .

A quiet stillness greeted his words
voices, questions, doubts
silenced for the moment
hesitancy and wonder mingled
reflected in their eyes
A wave, a nod to the man in grey
they left the room
promising to meet again

An afterword

Without a Second traces the path I am travelling, a step by step journey, through the vast field of Vedanta: A journey of not just discovery and wonder, but also of hesitation and doubts, those that I stumbled upon as I entered the teaching. With little knowledge of Sanskrit, no friends wishing to enter the path with me, my only recourse was to discuss the subject with others attending the lectures. The following months revealed one thing. I was not alone in my doubts and that there were many like me who were, to say the least, quite bewildered by the teaching. The more we discussed the more problems we encountered. Like a Rubik's cube, every twist, while appearing to solve one side, brought a fresh one on another. I had two options to resolve the doubts, either to teach or to write. With my knowledge of Vedanta, teaching was really a non-option. There was no other way out of this maze except to put down the questions in black and white and find answers to them. Without a Second is the result of this exercise.

The choice of writing in free verse was not conscious or deliberate. It suggested itself. Gathering a momentum of their own, the words appeared to obey the diktats of an invisible director, flowing in a manner that did not fit well within a prose format. The many examples, explanations and details of Vedanta that I had heard from Swami Dayananda Saraswati over the years gradually cohered to unfold the vision that is Without a Second. Months of repeated typing, reading, and editing finally culminated in a text, which I hope is easy flowing, clear and precise. There are no punctuations to mark the end of an idea or sentence. Letters in the upper case indicate the beginning of an idea or sentence, personal pronoun, the words signifying Brahman and 'Its' pronouns. Lower case letters are used for god and his attributes, except in one instance – the Lord. I have continued the traditional gender bias, using the masculine gender for god. The few Sanskrit words in the text are in italics. I have avoided the use of diacritical marks, since the words are simple and easy to pronounce.

Having said that, perhaps some explanation as to the format and the choice of words will clarify any doubts the reader may have, since the first response to the text could probably be one of surprise. Vedanta is a serious inquiry of reality, a hallowed, venerable subject. I felt that the simple conversation English will make it easy to read; a 'gentle' communication of the profound, without detracting from the subject matter. Those who are used to the traditional teaching methods of Vedanta may find the writing style rather informal. I hope that the explanations will allay their fears. The question and answer format gave me a lot of freedom to add and delete portions without disturbing the main body of the text. The number of persons in the discussion, their choice of clothes, has no particular significance. As for the reason for replacing Sanskrit wherever and whenever possible: First, I have limited knowledge of this classical language, and second, I believe there are quite a few among us who are resistant to the language. When I hear a lecture heavily peppered with Sanskrit words and terms, I find I am unable to understand or assimilate the facts unless I mentally translate the words, which means that in the process of translation, I miss a better part of the lecture. To avoid these mental gymnastics, I thought the choice of English-only would make it easier and clearer for Sanskrit-resistant readers. Another reason for replacing Sanskrit was to avoid a mechanical repetition of words and terms, those I had either vaguely understood or even misunderstood. I felt that the effort to choose the appropriate English words would ensure I understood the terms correctly.

The equivalents to specific Vedanta terms include the definition of Brahman. '*Satyam, jnanam, anantam*' is the 'Limitless Existence Consciousness' of the text. *Sat* is translated as Is-ness, Am-ness, Being and Existence, *jnanam* by knowledge or intelligence or Consciousness; while *anantam* is translated as Limitless, All Pervading and Eternal. Wherever intelligence and knowledge indicate Brahman, they are always preceded by 'Limitless'. Once Limitless was the choice for *anantam*, I needed an appropriate English word for Brahman. Words such as big or immense did not convey the spirit of Brahman. I looked elsewhere for an answer and came across these phrases: '*Adviteeyam Brahma*' (Brahman without a second) and '*tad ekam*' (It is One), the very words I was looking for. I chose Without a Second as the title and One to mean Brahman. However, One by itself did not adequately convey the sense of the absolute. Swamiji suggested that I add the word

Limitless. Brahman in the text is, therefore, the Limitless One. Not only Brahman, the Limitless One is the godhead that is Brahman with *maya*, which is the entire creation, both in the manifest and resolved state.

The next step was to find words for the ontological terms such as *satyam* and *mithya*. *Mithya* means something existing within time and space, constantly changing, not separate or 'other' than *satyam*, and without independent existence. It depends on and derives its existence from *satyam*. It includes the entire creation, including every thought, every concept or idea, everything known and unknown. I thought real *(satyam)* and dependent-real (*mithya*) conveyed the meaning more accurately and have explained the terms. Swamiji suggested that dependent-real, not being the perfect synonym for *mithya*, it would be better to use *mithya* along with dependent-real. He felt dependent-real was limited in its meaning and could be mistaken to be another parallel reality along with *satyam*. As far as possible, I have used the word *mithya* along with dependent-real. The other Sanskrit words are usually accompanied by English explanations, the words such as *dharma* (of the many meanings, it is order or harmony) and *ardha-nari* (male-female figure of Lord Siva).

As far as epistemology is concerned, 'Valid means of knowledge' replaces the Sanskrit word '*pramana*', literally 'by which we come to know'. The English equivalents for the Sanskrit terms are as follows: direct perception for *pramana*, inference for *anumana* and *arthapatti*, illustration for *upamana*, knowledge of absence for *anupalabdhi* and words for *shabda*. Although in Vedanta, *shabda* / words refer to the Vedas in general and to the *Upanishad*s in particular, it was difficult for me to accept them as a *pramana*. Like the questioners, I too felt I was mortgaging my mind and independent thinking by accepting others' words. Nor could I accept the Vedas as revealed texts. How could they be? After all, they were products of a human mind since they are in a human language. If I could accept the Vedas I should accept the other texts also. I needed to clarify my doubts and hence I have dealt with the topic rather extensively. As I wrote, it became increasingly clear to me that the *Upanishad*s is not only a valid means to know the 'knower' but is the only valid means. I cannot thank Swamiji adequately for making me understand the importance of the

Upanishads as *pramana*. It is nothing short of a discovery to realise that the key to know the truth of our real nature is to understand that the *Upanishads* are the *pramana*. Just as our five senses and our mind are indispensable to know and transact with the world, the *Upanishads* are indispensable to know the 'self', the *atma*.

The first five 'chapters' explain the terms 'limitless, existence, real, dependent-real or *mithya*, orders of reality, and cognition. The next six chapters discuss the validity of the Vedas, particularly the *Upanishads*, as means of knowledge, *pramana*, to know the truth of the *atma*, the 'self'. From *pramanas* to cause and effect and the creation brings the all-too-often-misunderstood question of *maya*. The following seventeen chapters explain these topics, particularly the ontology of *maya*; its role, the world as a superimposition or projection and the dependent-real status of the individual mind. In the final seventeen chapters, I have tried to answer some of the commonly asked questions which include the following: The importance of a master, is knowledge an experience or understanding, mysticism versus knowledge, compassion and Brahman's apparent indifference, fate or free-will, the qualifications of an ideal student, methods of practice and schools of thought, and the after death status of sages. It concludes with the wonder that is the knowledge of Without a Second.

Vedanta is a vast subject and the topics are innumerable. Each one of them can be analysed in great depth and detail to warrant a separate volume. However, as I said earlier, the book is a personal record of a neophyte's entry into Vedanta. As a result, Without a Second does not deal with the more complex aspects of the subject. Despite these constraints, I hope the reader finds the chosen topics comprehensive and relevant. And that the explanations whetted on the touchstone of *sruti* (*Upanishad*s), *yukti* (logic and reason), and *anubhava* (understanding), are logical, clear and precise.

Sheela Balaji
November 2004

The Story of the Eighteenth Elephant

A rich merchant bequeathed a herd of seventeen elephants to his three sons. He left one half of the herd to his eldest son, one third to his second son, while the youngest was to receive the rest. The problem, however, was in dividing the elephants according to the merchant's will. Naturally, a quarrel arose among the three, each claiming his share. Just then, the minister passed by, riding on his elephant. He enquired the reason for the quarrel. When the sons explained the reason, the minister said, "I will include my elephant in the herd and now we have eighteen elephants." Of course, the sons were delighted since they would be richer by one more animal. The minister continued, "One half of eighteen is nine; so you the eldest, please take them." The man drove away his herd, very pleased at the result. "You, the second son, one third of the herd is six and that is your share." The second man left with the animals. "Now, you, the youngest, your father left you seventeen elephants.

The first man has nine and the second has six. That makes fifteen in all. The remaining was to go to you and that means two and here are the two." The dispute resolved to everyone's satisfaction, the minister left, with his 'eighteenth' elephant.

Once we understand the truth of our 'self', *maya*, like the eighteenth elephant, has no further role.

Glossary

Absolute	Brahman
All Pervading	Sarva Gatam
Beginning-less	Anadi
Consciousness	Brahman, Chit
Deep Sleep State	Sushupti Avastha
Dependent – real	Mithya
Dream State	Swapna Avastha
Ego	Ahamkara
Empirical, Transactional Real	Vyavaharika Sat
Eternal	Nityam
Existence, Being, Is – ness	Sat
Fourth State	Turiya
Fruits of Action	Karma Phalam
God, Godhead	Ishwara
Happiness aspect	Anandamaya
I Am-ness, I sense	Aham Buddhi
I thought	Aham Vritti
Ignorance	Avidya
Insentient	Acetanam, Jadam
Intellect	Buddhi
Intelligent Maker	Nimitta Karanam
Knower	Pramata
Knowledge	Jnanam
Limitless	Anantam
Limitless Knowledge, Limitless Intelligence	Brahman
Limitless One, Limitless Consciousness	Brahman

Material, Matter	Upadanam
Maya	Maya
Maya of three kinds	Trigunatmika Maya
Memory	Cittam
Mind	Manas
Mind form, Mental frame	Vritti
Nothing – ness, Emptines	Shunyata
Non – Dual	Advaitam
Not I	Anatma
One	Brahman
Physical aspect	Annamaya
Physiological aspect	Pranamaya
Projection	Vikshepanam
Psychological aspect	Manomaya, Vijnanamaya
Real, Reality	Satyam
'Self'	Atma
Sentient	Cetanam
Spirit	Brahman
Subjective Real	Pratibhasika Sat
Superimposition, Projection	Aropa, Adhyasa
Supreme	Ishwara
The I	Pramata, Atma
Transcendental Real	Paramarthika Sat
Triple Knot of Ignorance	Avidya-Kama- Karma
Truth	Satyam
Valid Means of Knowledge	Pramanam
Veiling	Avaranam
Waking State	Jagrat Avastha

Without a Cause	Akaranam
Without a Second	Adviteeyam
All that is here is Brahman	Sarvam khalu idam brahma
I am the All Pervading One	Ayam atma brahma
The One is all knowledge	Prajnanam brahma
The One is Limitless Existence Consciousness	Satyam jnanam anantam brahma
Your are that	Tat tvam asi